WORD-WISE SOURCEBOOK™ ONE

for First and Second Grade Teachers

Laugh-Aloud Rhymes for
Learning Language Skills

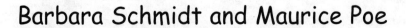

Your source for blackline master poems with
language-learning follow-up activity ideas to
extend the word explorations in Rebecca Sitton's
SPELLING SOURCEBOOK® Series.

Barbara Schmidt and Maurice Poe

About the Authors

Barbara Schmidt earned her doctorate in Curriculum and Instruction at the University of California, Berkeley. Dr. Schmidt is a Professor Emeritus of Language and Literacy at California State University, Sacramento, and has taught at the elementary levels in Pennsylvania, Washington, and California. She serves as a consultant in the areas of early childhood education and language development, and in all aspects of reading and language curriculum and instruction. Dr. Schmidt has authored several instructional publications in the areas of language and literacy. She is an active member of the International Reading Association and Past-President of the California Reading Association. Dr. Schmidt is a much sought after featured speaker at conferences and workshops throughout the United States.

Maurice Poe earned his doctorate in Curriculum and Instruction/Psychology at the University of Oregon. Dr. Poe is a Professor of Language and Literacy in the School of Education at California State University, Sacramento, and teaches pre-service and graduate classes in language and literacy. He has also taught at the elementary and secondary levels, accruing over 30 years experience in education. Dr. Poe is the Past-President of the Sacramento Area Reading Association and has authored several instructional publications in the areas of language and literacy.

"Ten Little Monkeys" by Barbara Schmidt and Maurice Poe. From *Willie MacGurkle and Friends*. Copyright 1987 by Curriculum Associates, Inc. Selection reprinted by permission of the publisher.

"One Shoe, Two Shoes" by Barbara Schmidt and Maurice Poe. From *Reading Rhythms Book 1*. Copyright 1994 by Steck-Vaughn Company. Selection reprinted by permission of the publisher.

"The Animals Have the Sillies Today" and "Macaroni" by Barbara Schmidt and Maurice Poe. From *Reading Rhythms Book 2*. Copyright 1994 Steck-Vaughn Company. Selections reprinted by permission of the publisher.

Illustrator: Donna Bernard

ISBN 1-886050-46-5
©1997, 2003—Egger Publishing, Inc.
P.O. Box 12248, Scottsdale, AZ 85267
Phone: 480-596-5100 FAX: 480-951-2276
Toll Free: 888-937-7355 (888-WE-SPELL)
www.sittonspelling.com

TABLE OF CONTENTS

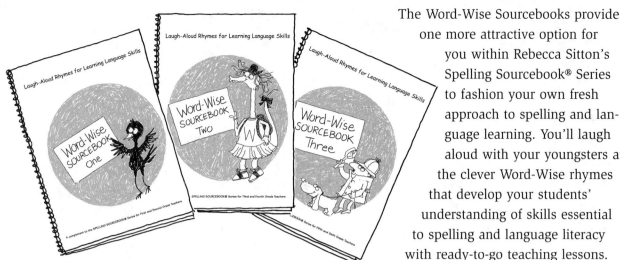

The Word-Wise Sourcebooks provide one more attractive option for you within Rebecca Sitton's Spelling Sourcebook® Series to fashion your own fresh approach to spelling and language learning. You'll laugh aloud with your youngsters at the clever Word-Wise rhymes that develop your students' understanding of skills essential to spelling and language literacy with ready-to-go teaching lessons.

This book, **Word-Wise Sourcebook™ One**, has been created for you to use with first and second grade students—the topics support concepts in Levels 1 and 2 of the Spelling Sourcebook Series. *Word-Wise Sourcebook Two* follows for grades 3–4 with topics that parallel learning in Levels 3 and 4. Finally, *Word-Wise Sourcebook Three* for grades 5–6 augments Levels 5 and 6 of the Spelling Sourcebook Series.

The Word-Wise Sourcebooks complement Levels 1–6 of the Spelling Sourcebook Series, but are not tied to specific units or lessons in the Series. Further, the Word-Wise Sourcebooks can be used independently of the Spelling Sourcebook Series to enhance and liven any spelling program.

For more information on the Spelling Sourcebook Series for grades 1–8:	
Read about the Series in this book	Page 87
Call Egger Publishing, Inc.	Toll-free 888-WE-SPELL (937-7355)
Visit our Web site	www.sittonspelling.com
Request a free Overview Video that explains the Series and shows teachers using it in their classrooms	Toll-free 888-WE-SPELL (937-7355) www.sittonspelling.com
Attend a seminar in your area	Toll-free 888-WE-SPELL (937-7355) www.sittonspelling.com
Schedule your own seminar with a certified trainer of the Spelling Sourcebook Series	Toll-free 888-WE-SPELL (937-7355)
Contact the author, Rebecca Sitton	Home: 480-473-7277 Office: toll-free 888-WE-SPELL (937-7355) Email: rsitton@sittonspelling.com
Order a copy of the Spelling Sourcebook for your grade level	Order form, last page

You may think I'm just a funny bird,
But teachers, let me share a word
Or two about what I can do
To help you and your students, too!

Dear Teachers,

You are the bridge builders—the engineers who construct a strong connection between oral language and print for your young learners. Your task is critical and challenging. You deserve some help: Wordy Birdy to the rescue!

In *Word-Wise Sourcebook One,* we have crafted 32 lessons, each introducing or reinforcing a key word element, a spelling generalization, or a vocabulary skill. Each lesson begins with a concrete teaching example followed by a read-aloud poem that humorously focuses attention on the topic. Wordy Birdy, the sometimes confused class mascot, helps to initiate each lesson and stays around as students get their own blackline master copy of the poem for shared reading and guided practice. Because this program has been designed to meet the diverse needs of your young students, each lesson suggests developmentally appropriate extensions and applications that allow you to differentiate instruction for students who range from emerging to fluent.

The instructional sequence for each lesson is the same. Every lesson begins with explicit direct instruction that focuses and engages students in the skill in **INTO**, proceeds to the shared reading and guided practice in **THROUGH**, and culminates in strategy suggestions for applying the element or skill in **BEYOND**. Masters for helpful and appealing puppets are provided that will help coach students over and around some of the major stumbling blocks of print.

Word-Wise Sourcebook One has also been designed to meet your needs. Each lesson is meant to complement any curriculum that you presently use. Whether used to introduce, reinforce, offer practice, reteach, or assess a particular skill, the lessons provide learning experiences that are hands-on and heads-on: students are actively engaged in thinking and doing.

Teachers who have used Wordy and his poems in their classrooms suggest that the activities offer ideal portfolio data. They often make a "home" for Wordy Birdy in a large carton where duplicated copies are organized in manila folders according to the particular skill being introduced. Since Wordy's program directly speaks to the most challenging word elements, teachers may add more teaching techniques to their Word-Wise Sourcebook files.

You may want to put Wordy's rhymes on charts, underlining <u>examples</u> of the word elements. These charts can serve as visual reminders for your students. You may choose to make Wordy Birdy puppets for your students so that they have a comforting buddy when you are working with words. There is no limit to the creative ways in which you and your students can flexibly adapt this Word-Wise Sourcebook to meet your needs.

Wordy is eagerly waiting to invade your classroom with laughter, language, and learning. Enjoy!

Warm regards,
The Authors

Barbara Maurice

Barbara   Maurice   Wordy Birdy

LESSON 1
Introduction: Wordy Birdy

Wordy Birdy

My name is Wordy Birdy.
    I'm not like other birds.
They can sing and chirp and tweet,
    But I can play with WORDS!
That's why I'm Wordy Birdy.
    Just watch what I can do.
Follow me—if I can do it,
    You can do it, too!

INTO

Wordy Birdy is the mascot who leads you and your students into learning and laughter with language. With this rhyme, introduce Wordy Birdy to students as you explore some of Wordy's adventures with words.

Make your own Wordy Birdy puppet using the template provided on Puppet Master 1. Some puppet possibilities might be affixing Wordy to a popsicle stick, a construction-paper finger ring, a brown paper sack, or whatever works for you. Feathers help! As class mascot, Wordy Birdy can help you focus students' attention on any of your lessons dealing with concepts of print, phonemic awareness, decoding strategies, and vocabulary.

You may choose to have students make their own Wordy Birdy puppet to use as they work with letters and words. Puppets may be kept in students' folders.

THROUGH

Introduce the new member of your class—Wordy Birdy—who is especially good at doing something. Ask students to listen to find out what Wordy Birdy can do. Read the poem aloud several times so that students can chime in. Engage students in discussing Wordy Birdy's talent.

Distribute copies of Blackline Master 1. Ask students to follow along, join in, and identify key words as you guide them through several choral readings.

Call attention to the illustration of Wordy Birdy next to the poem. Ask students what they think Wordy will do when he plays with words.

Have students look at Wordy Birdy's request for help in the middle of the page as you read aloud: *Your turn! Help me make new words!* Guide students through writing the initial consonant to complete the word that names each picture. Compare the word endings.

BEYOND

Wordy's rhyme can introduce any working-with-words lesson from your regular curriculum, or you might have students do the following:

1. **Meeting Wordy:** Model a way introductions can be made. Carefully print Wordy Birdy's name on a name tag. Suggest to students that since Wordy will be with them for a while, he wants to learn their names. Have students make their own name tag and introduce themselves to Wordy by saying, "Hello, Wordy. My name is _____. This is the word that names who I am." Discuss some features of names: left to right, names of letters, sounds of letters, silent letters, etc.

2. **Follow Wordy Birdy:** Be ready with a marking pen, tape, and paper labels as Wordy Birdy leads you around the room. When you make Wordy Birdy stop and point to an object, students will call out the name of that object so that you can make and affix a label.

3. **Journal:** Ask students to draw their version of Wordy Birdy in their journal or on separate paper. Explain what a "talk bubble" is. Have students make a talk bubble coming out of Wordy's mouth and fill the bubble with words he might be saying.

LESSON 2
Labeling Objects:
Words Around the Room

INTO

Explain that Wordy Birdy wants to do TWO things: Wordy wants to learn some new words AND Wordy also wants to be able to find things in the room. If students are wearing name tags or have name tags at their seats, remind them that Wordy can find them because of labels that tell their name. If things around the room are labeled, Wordy can tell what things are and find each one.

Demonstrate how to make a new label for something in the room: **flag**, **soccer ball**, **clock**, **telephone**, etc. Reinforce the concept of letters, sounds, and words by thinking out loud as you label: "Let's see, now . . . if I want to write the word for ＿＿, I need to think of the letter(s) that makes the sound at the beginning of the word and then I have to. . . ." Ask a student to place the label where it belongs as the class **reads** the word.

THROUGH

Tell students to listen carefully as you read this lesson's poem to see if they can figure out what Wordy is telling them to do. Read the poem aloud several times. Engage students in discussing the difference between *counting* the words and *knowing* the words.

> **Words Around the Room**
> Walk around the room with me.
> Count how many words you see!
> Walking fast or walking slow,
> What really **counts** are words you **know**!

Distribute copies of Blackline Master 2. Ask students to follow along, join in, and identify key words as you guide them through several choral readings.

Call attention to Wordy Birdy's actions in the illustration next to the poem by asking students: What is wrong with this picture? Ask students to help correct Wordy's mislabeling.

Lead students on a "Counting March" around the room, counting all the labels. Then ask students to find and stand beside a label that they know. Have students say: "I know that this is a ＿＿ because the label says ＿＿."

Direct students' attention to Wordy's talk bubble and read what Wordy asks. Note the two empty boxes and lines for labels. Direct students to choose any two items in the room to draw and label, either already-labeled items or things they can try to label themselves. Provide time for students to share their labeled pictures.

BEYOND

This rhyme can be an effective lead-in for other working-with-words lessons, or you might reinforce the concept of labels with the following:

1. **Look at the Labels:** Ask students to bring in labels from everyday items (cereal boxes, canned foods, toothpaste tubes, clothes labels, etc.) for a bulletin board display or table collection. Discuss information on the labels.

2. **Make Your Own Label:** Ask students to *think up* something new: a new ice-cream flavor, a new toy, a new imaginary friend, etc. Have them draw a picture of their creation and give it a new-name label.

3. **Fix It Up:** Rearrange labels on items in the classroom while students are out of the room. Ask for volunteers to do a *fix-up* and put labels back on appropriate objects.

LESSON 3
Initial Consonants:
Pick a Letter

INTO

This lesson assumes that you have already introduced your students to the alphabet and that students have some knowledge of the two important concepts of letters: letters have names and letters "make" sounds. Perhaps you have used your students' names to reinforce the concept that letters can be put together to form a word. In this rhyme, Wordy Birdy will guide students by reinforcing both names of letters and the sounds those letters represent at the beginning of words.

THROUGH

Announce to students that Wordy Birdy is very excited. Wordy has learned to recognize all the letters in the alphabet, and now he can figure out the letters that begin new words. Ask students to listen to find out what Wordy Birdy can do. Read the poem aloud several times. Engage students in discussing Wordy Birdy's newly found talent.

Pick a Letter

Wordy Birdy picked a **b**
 For babies, bananas, and bats,
Flew next door and picked a **c**
 For coconuts, candy, and cats.

Your turn now to pick a letter,
 Think of words that start the same.
Wordy knows you're getting better
 At this Wordy Birdy game!

Distribute copies of Blackline Master 3. Ask students to follow along, join in, and identify key words as you guide them through several choral readings.

Call attention to Wordy Birdy's picture in the illustration next to the poem. Ask students to describe what Wordy is showing them. Have students find the talk bubble where Wordy says: *"Your turn! Make pictures to match each beginning letter."* Have students draw pictures of words starting with **b** and **d**. You may wish to guide students through this activity or have them complete the activity at their seats.

BEYOND

This rhyme is a natural lead-in for further instruction in initial consonant letters and sounds. These activities provide additional practice:

1. **Clap for Sounds:** Have one student at a time select any letter from the alphabet. Given that letter, you will call out words that do or do not begin with that letter and sound. Students are to clap if the word begins with the appropriate sound; students are to sit on their hands if the word does not begin with the appropriate sound. This activity is a good check for phonemic awareness.

2. **Name Game:** Have students print their first name at the top of 8½" x 11" construction paper. Ask students to identify the letter and sound at the beginning of their name. Have them draw or search in magazines or catalogs for pictures of things that begin with the same letter and sound as their name. Encourage them to create a paper collage.

3. **Making a Pictionary:** Distribute multi-colored 11" x 24" sheets of construction paper to collaborative groups of three students. Each sheet will have a letter printed in the upper right-hand corner in upper and lower case. Students are to draw or search for and cut out pictures of things beginning with that letter for the purpose of creating their illustrated page for the class pictionary.

LESSON 4
Short Vowels: Which Sound Do You Hear?

 **INTO**

As with the lesson focusing on initial consonants, this lesson assumes that students have been introduced to the alphabet and have some knowledge of letter names and letter sounds. Select student first or last names that contain short vowel sounds (conform to a cvc pattern) and write those names on the board (Pat, Ron, Beth, etc.). Underline the vowel that represents the short vowel sound and pronounce the name; have students say the name aloud, listening to the sound of the underlined vowel. Ask students to identify the short vowel sound in each name by saying the sound aloud (**e: eh, eh**).

THROUGH

Tell students that Wordy Birdy is excited because he has some friends with interesting names and he wants students to meet his friends. Ask students to listen to the names of Wordy's friends and to what each of his friends is doing. Read the poem aloud several times using the letter sounds for each vowel.

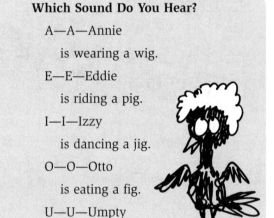

Which Sound Do You Hear?
A—A—Annie
   is wearing a wig.
E—E—Eddie
   is riding a pig.
I—I—Izzy
   is dancing a jig.
O—O—Otto
   is eating a fig.
U—U—Umpty
   is holding a twig.

Write **A E I O U** on the board and ask students to recall the name of Wordy's friend that corresponds to each of the vowels. Write the name under the appropriate vowel. Explain why you are using a BIG letter at the beginning of each name. Ask students to recall what each character was doing in the poem. (*Annie was wearing a wig; Eddie was riding a pig;* etc.).

Distribute copies of Blackline Master 4. Have students follow along and join in as you guide them through several choral readings.

Call attention to the illustration. Ask students what Wordy is doing and why. Ask students which character in the poem is doing the funniest thing and why it is funny. Have students find Wordy's talk bubble and follow along as you read: *"Your turn! Write the vowel **a**, **e**, **i**, **o**, or **u** to spell the words in each sentence."* Ask students to restate what Wordy is asking them to do. Call attention to the pictures of the fat cat and the bug in the rug and have students describe what they see. Tell students that pictures help us understand better what we're reading and that these pictures will help them figure out the missing vowels they need to write to complete the sentences.

 BEYOND

This rhyme introduces or reinforces the short vowel sounds that most often occur when the vowel appears between two consonants (cvc). The following activities provide additional practice with short vowel sounds:

1. **Do You Hear Me?** Write the character names from the poem on the board, underlining the beginning vowel: **Annie**; **Eddie**; **Izzy**; **Otto**; **Umpty**. Review the names of the characters and the short vowel sound at the beginning of each name. Slowly and deliberately read aloud words that contain short, long, and irregular vowel sounds. When students hear a short vowel sound, they are to call out the name of the character that represents that vowel sound: *hard, ant (Annie!), bold, odd (Otto!),* etc.

2. **Match My Vowel:** Reproduce or have students reproduce the vowels and the names of the characters from the poem on 3" x 5" cards: **a—Annie; e—Eddie; i—Izzy; o—Otto; u—Umpty**. As you read aloud words that begin with or contain short vowel sounds, students will hold up the card (from the five cards in front of them) that corresponds to the short vowel in the word you read aloud. Have a student read from a list of short vowel words while you observe students' responses.

3. **Vowel Couplets:** Write the following lines of a poem on the board, an overhead, or a worksheet, and invite students to supply the missing vowel in the incomplete words. After students have completed the activity, have them take turns reading the poem aloud in pairs, in small groups, or as a class.

> I like the **a** in t __ n
> and the **a** in f __ n.
> I like the **e** in p __ t
> and the **e** in n __ t.
> I like the **i** in s __ p
> and the **i** in r __ p.
> I like the **o** in h __ p
> and the **o** in p __ p.
> I like the **u** in g __ m
> and the **u** in h __ m.

LESSON 5
Family Names:
All in the Family

 INTO

The concept of family appears time and time again in the literature we share with young children and in children's daily oral and written expression. Since "family" is already an integral part of your curriculum, the poem and activities in this lesson can complement other learning experiences. Wordy Birdy is eager to introduce his family to your students and to have them introduce their families. Consider that many children have creative names for family members and these could be added to the list. Your students may describe a non-traditional family.

Encourage the description of alternative family groups and the inclusion of friends and pets in the family circle.

Prepare word cards for the following words: **mom, dad, brother, sister, grandma, grandpa, aunt, uncle, cousin, pet, friend**. These cards should be placed on a ledge in full view.

 THROUGH

Tell students Wordy is so excited he can hardly keep still because he wants the class to meet his family today. Ask students to look at the word cards to see if there are any names they know. Explain why you added **friend** and **pet** to the list of family members. Ask if students have any good friends or pets in their family. Ask students to join you in reading each of the word cards. Tell them to listen carefully to discover who belongs to Wordy's family. Read the poem aloud several times.

> **All in the Family**
>
> Please come to meet my family,
> Mom and Grandma and Auntie Bee!
> Look over here—four more to see,
> My uncle, my cousin, my brother, and me!

Have students find the word cards that identify Wordy's family members.

Distribute copies of Blackline Master 5. Have students identify key words as you guide them through several choral readings.

Call attention to the picture of Wordy's family under the poem. Discuss appropriate word cards for each family member. Focus students' attention on the words in Wordy's talk bubble. Read *"I want to meet your family"* aloud together. Explain that students are to draw a picture of their own family and use words to tell who each family member is so that Wordy can meet everyone. When pictures are completed, provide time for students to introduce their families to Wordy.

 BEYOND

The following activities reinforce family names as your students extend their writing skills:

1. **Family Names:** Explain to students that many people use other words when talking about their dad, mom, grandma, and grandpa. Tape four word cards labeled **dad, mom, grandma,** and **grandpa** across the board. Explain that some people call their dad *papa*. Write **papa** under **dad**. Encourage students to think of other possible labels for their dad: *daddy, father, pop*. Do the same with other family words. This is a good way to encourage acceptance of diversity among your students.

2. **Family Circle:** Distribute large sheets of colored construction paper with a drawing of a large circle. Write "My Family Circle" on the board. Have students copy these words at the top of their paper. Show students an example of your own family circle with pictures that you have drawn or photographs of family members pasted around the family circle. Each picture is labeled with a relationship word for the individual. Suggest that students ask their families at home to help with the Family Circle activity. Make a Family Circle bulletin board display.

3. **All in the Family Poem:** Put the following poem frame on the board:

   > Please come to meet my family.
   > ____ and ____ and ____!
   > Look over here — ____ more to see,
   > My ____, my ____, my ____, and me!

   Call attention to the similarity of the poem pattern to the poem students have just read. Explain that Wordy would be very happy to have students write their own family poems. Have the word cards with family words displayed for reference as students copy and complete the poem. These poems could be laminated for use as placemats.

LESSON 6
Word Families: Word Family Friends

INTO

This lesson introduces your students to the concept of phonetically regular words with similar ending patterns *(rimes)*. Now that your students have practiced names and sounds of individual consonants and vowels, they are ready to combine these letters and sounds into short word families. This lesson focuses on words that use the short sound of **a** in the medial position (short **a** is one of the most productive phonemes).

> Wordy Birdy knows that the study of high-frequency spelling patterns, or rimes, is a sensible, research-based strategy to generate hundreds of words. Several respected educators (including Wylie and Durrell, Edward Fry, and Marilyn Adams) have identified 35-40 rimes that can form up to 650 different one-syllable primary words. These key rimes are taught and recycled continuously through the first two levels of the Spelling Sourcebook Series and then occur intermittently for reinforcement at subsequent levels. The activities in this lesson complement this practice.

Remind students of a previous lesson in which they met Wordy's family and introduced Wordy to their own family. Explain that Wordy is very excited today because he has some **other** families that he wants students to meet.

Write **an** on the board. Tell students that the **an** family is one that Wordy wants them to meet. Explain that this is a big family and that the names of all the members of the family end in **an** but begin with a different letter. Ask students to look carefully at the letters of the alphabet to find letters that make a word with **an**. If needed, model by choosing **g** and writing **g a n** under **an**. Shake your head as you tell students that **gan** cannot belong to the **an** family because it is not a word. Write **r a n** under **an**, asking students if this is a word. Encourage students to try other letters and list their words in the **an** family.

THROUGH

Explain that students will be meeting many new word families that will help them read and write. Ask them to listen carefully to Wordy's poem to hear about some of these families. Read the poem aloud several times.

> **Word Family Friends**
>
> Come over to meet the **an** family,
>
> Here's **m** and **r** and **c**.
>
> And next to them is the **at** family,
>
> Here's **c** and **f** and **b**.
>
> Be sure to meet the **ap** family,
>
> Here's **m** and **c** and **t**.
>
> It's fun to meet word families,
>
> How many can you see?

Refer to the board to review the **an** family from your previous discussion. Use the board to illustrate the other families and their word members. Explain that Wordy thinks it's a pretty good trick that all the words in a family look and sound the same at the end.

Distribute copies of Blackline Master 6. Have students follow along and join in as you guide them through several choral readings.

Call attention to the picture next to the poem. Ask students why each bird is holding a letter.

Read aloud Wordy's talk bubble: *"Your turn! Write the name of each family member you met under its house."* Show students that one family member has already been listed in each column. Ask students what they will need to look at to write the names of the other family members. This activity may be done independently or in groups.

 BEYOND

This lesson introduces the concept of similarly patterned word endings. You may want to continue introducing two-letter families with a medial vowel (**-et, -eg, -en, -id, -im, -ip, -ig, -it, -ix, -ot, -op, -og, -od, -ut, -un, -ug**) before you move to three-letter combinations (**-eet, -ish, -oot, -and, -art, -arm, -ark, -old, -ell, -ill**, etc.). These activities provide practice with word families:

1. **Family of the Day:** In a special place on the board, put a word ending under the label **Today's Family.** Have skinny strips of lined paper available so that students can complete an independent seat assignment by writing as many family names as they can by the end of the school day.

2. **Mail Delivery:** Have students make three or four "mailboxes" out of shoe boxes. Tape a word ending to each box. Pass out "postcards" so students can write the names of family members and insert the cards in the appropriate mail slots. This activity can also be used for "delivering" rhyming words, synonyms, or any other appropriate word elements.

3. **Family Circles:** Put three or four familiar word endings on index cards, string each one on yarn, and select students to wear these word-family necklaces. Have one student stand in each corner of the room. Assign a team of students to each word family. Students must write an appropriate word on a card in order to line up behind the head of the family. This might be a good way to line up for recess!

LESSON 7
Rhyming Words:
Don't Call Me
Wordy Piggy

 INTO

Introduce or reinforce the concept of rhyming words by asking students to turn on their best listening by gently tugging three times on each earlobe. This means they are ready for the "sharp ears" game! Tell students that you will try to trick them by writing a word on the board and then calling out some other words. If the words you call out rhyme with the word on the board, students give a "thumbs up"; if not, "thumbs down." Select three or four easy-to-rhyme familiar words for the game.

 THROUGH

Ask students why they think Wordy is called "Wordy Birdy" instead of "Wordy Chick" or "Wordy Bird." After they have determined that Wordy's two names rhyme, explain that Wordy is very proud of his rhyming name. Have students listen to the lesson's poem to find out why Wordy has a rhyming name. Read the poem aloud several times. Discuss how Wordy got his name.

Don't Call Me Wordy Piggy

Please don't call me **Wordy Piggy**!
That is not this birdy's name.
My mama said my name should be
Two words that sound the same.

Please don't call me **Birdy Yellow**,
Or **Wordy Once-Upon-A-Time**.
You must call me **Wordy Birdy**,
'Cause then my name will rhyme!

Distribute copies of Blackline Master 7. Have students follow along, join in, and identify key words as you guide them through several choral readings.

Call attention to Wordy Birdy's actions in the illustration next to the poem. Ask students what they think Wordy is trying to do. Have students find the talk bubble in which Wordy says: *"Your turn! Pick an animal word that makes a rhyme. Then draw a picture of your animal in the box."* Call attention to the two empty boxes and the labels below the boxes. Explain that students need to think of an animal word that rhymes to finish the label. Ask students which animal has a name that sounds like *funny.* Have students close their eyes and listen to each response to judge whether or not the name rhymes with *funny.* If they have difficulty coming up with *bunny,* give them some clues. You may choose to guide students through this activity and have them complete the pictures on their own.

 **BEYOND**

This lesson is a natural lead-in to further identification of rhyming words and sounds. The following activities provide practice with rhyming words:

1. **Find a Rhyme Time:** Call out simple jingles, nursery rhymes, and familiar poems omitting the appropriate rhyming word. Ask students to fill in the rhyme. Write the words that rhyme on the board. Have students identify the discriminating features that make these words rhyme. Warn them that not all rhyming words look alike.

2. **Pick-A-Stick:** From a can of popsicle sticks or tongue depressors, have volunteers "Pick-A-Stick" and use it to point to rhyming words as you chorally read familiar charts and chants.

3. **Make a Rhyme:** As students recall color words, write them on the board. Ask students to fold plain paper into quarters. Have them select any four color words from the board to make a rhyming-word match in each quarter. For example: green bean; blue shoe; red bed. Remind students that their rhyming words may have different spellings, but that they are to search for words that *sound* alike.

LESSON 8
Color Words:
Color Me Pink

 INTO

Your classroom is already exploding with color and offers many opportunities to reinforce color words, but for Wordy Birdy and some of your students, these words may need extra attention. *Color Me Pink* can be used to introduce any activity that offers practice in color words. Explain that Wordy Birdy sometimes mixes up words like *blue* and *black* because they look alike at the beginning.

 <u>THROUGH</u>

 <u>BEYOND</u>

Tell students that Wordy needs practice with color words—and that's not **all** Wordy needs! Ask students to listen to Wordy Birdy's color rhyme to find out why his mother was angry with him. Read the poem aloud several times.

RED BERRY JAM

Color Me Pink

Wordy fell into the bathtub.

Wordy fell into the sink.

Wordy fell into the cherry jam

And came out **pink**!

Wordy fell into the bucket.

Wordy fell into the bed.

Wordy fell into the berry jam

And came out **red**!

Discuss how Wordy got into trouble.

Distribute copies of Blackline Master 8. Encourage students to follow along, join in, and identify key words as you guide them through several choral readings. Ask students why Wordy came out **pink** in one part of the poem and **red** in the other.

Call attention to the sorry sight of Wordy Birdy climbing out of the red berry jam. Discuss why he looks so unhappy.

Read aloud what Wordy is saying at the bottom of the page. Explain that Wordy has just finished painting the top of the big can of black paint. Ask students how they can help Wordy learn the colors of the paint in the other cans. Provide time for students to color and share their papers.

Color Me Pink can serve as an introduction to color word activities. Its repetition of simple words and sentences as well as its vivid images make it a natural laugh-getter for your young students. If additional experiences with color words are needed, try any of the following:

1. **Match a Color:** Label pockets of a pocket chart with color words or make construction paper pockets on a piece of poster board and label each pocket with a color word. Prepare construction paper strips of each color. After you have read aloud each color word, invite students to select a color strip, read the appropriate color word, and place the color strip in the appropriate pocket. This makes an ideal center activity.

2. **Make a Color Collage:** Ask students to select a favorite color of construction paper. Suggest that they use pictures cut from magazines and catalogs to make a collage of this color. Have students label their finished collage with the appropriate color word. The collages make an attractive bulletin board display.

3. **Rainbow Painting:** Have students create a rainbow with paint or crayons. Ask them to write the colors in their rainbow beneath their drawing.

Wordy Birdy likes to use My Spell Check to help him spell color words. See page 87. (Order form, last page.)

LESSON 9
Counting Words: Monkeying Around

 INTO

Students will enter your classroom with different levels of concept awareness. While many may recognize that *two monkeys* matches the numeral 2, some students may need additional reinforcement. *Monkeying Around* offers a rhythmic and appealing introduction to activities using counting words.

 **THROUGH**

Explain that in this Wordy Birdy rhyme, Wordy is trying to count little monkeys. Ask students to count in their heads the number of monkeys they hear counted in the poem. Read the poem aloud several times.

Monkeying Around

One little monkey tying her shoe;
Along came another,
And then there were two.

Two little monkeys drinking some tea;
Along came another,
And then there were three.

Three little monkeys banging on a door;
Along came another,
And then there were four.

Discuss the number of monkeys and their activities.

Distribute copies of Blackline Master 9. Have students follow along, join in, and identify key words as you guide them through several choral readings.

Call attention to Wordy in the illustration next to the poem. Ask students to tell what they think is happening.

Read aloud Wordy's talk bubble: *"Your turn! Help me count these monkeys."* Explain that students will need to count very carefully so that they can write the number word opposite each group of monkeys.

Wordy Birdy likes to use My Spell Check to help him spell number words. See page 87. (Order form, last page.)

 **BEYOND**

Add this poem to your repertoire of counting poems, songs, and chants. The poem offers a simple pattern for creating additional original stanzas. The following activities may prove useful:

1. **Show-and-Tell:** Divide your students into pairs. Give each pair ten 1" x 1" squares of construction paper. Demonstrate how students will write the numerals 1–10, one per square, and the appropriate number word on the other side of each square. Each student can make five squares. Distribute ten beans or similar counting objects to each team. One team member holds up a counting word. The other member must show the number of beans that matches the word. The numeral can be used as a check for understanding. Then players switch roles. Have students save their number cards in an envelope for other activities.

2. **Roll-And-Tell:** Divide your class into pairs of students. Have each pair use one set of number cards. Distribute one die to each

team. One member rolls the die; the second member holds up the appropriate word card.

3. **Make-A-Rhyme:** Using the "One little monkey…" pattern, ask students to help Wordy make a new rhyme. Put the following sentence frames on the board:

> Four little monkeys out for a _____;
> Along came another, and then there were _____.

This same pattern can be used with numbers six through ten. If time permits, students might copy individual stanzas, arrange themselves in numerical order, and recite their poem.

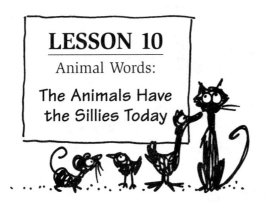

LESSON 10
Animal Words:
The Animals Have the Sillies Today

 INTO

Much of the literature for young learners—stories, poems, and chants—features animals. Animals also often appear in young children's writing. *The Animals Have the Sillies Today* is a whimsical introduction to developing and reinforcing student recognition and use of animal words.

 THROUGH

Announce to students that Wordy Birdy is excited about this lesson's poem. He wants everyone to meet his friends in the animal world.

But today his animal friends are being silly. Ask students to listen to the poem to find out how they are being silly. Read the poem aloud several times.

The Animals Have the Sillies Today

The animals have
   The sillies today.
The animals talk
   In the funniest way.

"Peep," says the duck.
"Squeak," says the cat.
"Quack," says the chick.
"Meow," says the rat.

Review the names of the animals in the poem. Discuss their unusual behavior.

Distribute copies of Blackline Master 10. Have students follow along, join in, and identify key words as you guide them through several choral readings.

Ask individual students to make the sounds of the animals in the poem.

Call attention to Wordy in the illustration next to the poem. Why is Wordy looking so upset? Have students identify the animals in the four boxes. Are these the same animals that are in the poem? Go over the sounds that these four animals are making in the poem. Then have students provide the appropriate sounds for each of the animals.

Call attention to Wordy's talk bubble: *"Your turn! Let's help these silly animals. Put the right sound in each talk bubble and the animal name on the line."* Ask students to explain what Wordy wants them to do with the talk bubbles and empty lines. Students can complete the page independently or with a partner.

 **BEYOND**

Use this rhyme to introduce activities with animal names. For additional experience, point out the seventeen animal names on students' My Spell Check (see page 87). For more practice, try any of the following activities:

1. **Story Theater:** Write the names of the animals in the poem on four index cards. Use yarn to make a necklace with each card. Choose four students to wear the character cards as they role play. As you narrate the poem, each student will act out and make the sound of his or her animal. You may also choose to have students write the poem, putting in the appropriate sound of their animal.

2. **Animal Study:** Begin a matrix chart that has animal names in a list on the left side and common categories of animal life across the top (sounds, habitat, color, food, skin, etc). Unique characteristics of animals can be listed on this chart as students study the animals in the curriculum.

3. **Match the Sound:** Arrange word cards with familiar animal names along the chalk ledge. Ask for a volunteer to make the distinctive sound of an animal. Choose another student to find the appropriate animal card that matches the animal sound.

Wordy Birdy and all his friends are learning to spell the names of their favorite animals. They use My Spell Check. See page 87. (Order form, last page.)

LESSON 11
Food Words:
Macaroni

 INTO

You may have already involved your students in words that name food, such as those listed on My Spell Check (see page 87). After all, food is not only good to eat but it's fun to talk about, read about, and write about. This lesson's poem offers easy access into the wonderful world of food. As usual, Wordy is having a problem—his own favorite food is *"Messy as can be!"*

 **THROUGH**

Explain to students that Wordy has a favorite food. Ask students to think of their most favorite food and name it as you write the list on a chart. Add the word *macaroni* to the chart, telling students that this is Wordy's favorite food. Discuss macaroni with your students. If possible, bring in some cooked macaroni for students to touch and taste. Discuss how it looks and tastes. Ask students to listen to find out what problem Wordy has with his favorite food. Read the poem aloud several times. Discuss Wordy's problem.

Macaroni

Macaroni, macaroni,

That's the stuff for me.

Macaroni, macaroni,

Messy as can be.

Distribute copies of Blackline Master 11. Ask students to follow along, join in, and identify

19

key words as you guide them through several choral readings.

Call attention to Wordy in the illustration next to the poem. Ask students if Wordy is enjoying his food and if he is making a mess. Call attention to the talk bubble and read Wordy's request: *"Your turn! Think of your favorite messy food. Make a picture of it in this box."* Ask students to think of some of the messiest foods they love to eat. Explain that they are to draw a picture of their favorite messy food in the empty box. Tell students that they will write their own favorite messy food poem on the lines beneath the box.

Referring to the chart of favorite foods, ask students to add any other favorite foods that are especially messy. Select one of the foods and model the sentence frame to create a new messy foods poem (e.g., *Hot dogs, hot dogs, That's the stuff for me.*). Provide time for students to share their drawings and poems.

Wordy Birdy likes to eat the foods listed on My Spell Check (see page 87). Sometimes he writes silly stories about eating banana pizzas or cake sandwiches!

 **BEYOND**

You will use the chart of favorite foods for many thinking and writing activities. Here are a few possibilities:

1. **Picture Words:** Give each student a 3" x 3" square of construction paper. Ask students to draw a picture of their favorite food from the food words chart. When pictures are complete, collect and redistribute them to the class. Ask for volunteers to match the picture they received to the appropriate word on the chart. Tape the pictures to the chart or put the chart and pictures at a learning station.

2. **Writing Sentences:** Put the following sentence frame on the board: *I like _____ because _____.* Demonstrate how you would fill in the sentence to make it complete. Distribute lined paper so that students can compose their own sentences using words from the favorite foods chart.

3. **Categorizing:** Ask students to fold their lined paper into two halves. Demonstrate putting a simple smiling face at the top of one half and a frowning face at the top of the other half. Ask students where they will write the names of foods they like and where they will write the names of foods they do not like. Suggest that they list at least three foods in each column. Food words can be categorized in many ways for additional practice: hot foods/cold foods; foods we eat with our fingers/foods we eat with utensils; junk foods/healthy foods; breakfast/lunch/dinner foods; etc.

LESSON 12
Nouns:
Who Thinks Up Names?

 INTO

Introduce the concept of words that name things (nouns) by making three columns on the board labeled: **People**, **Places**, and **Things**. Pick the name of a student in class and write that student's name in column 1. Ask students what would happen if everybody in the room had that same name: What problems would we have on the playground and in our class? Encourage students to see that people have their own unique names. Explain that **places**, pointing to column 2, also have their own names. Ask students what problems there would be if all cities and towns had the same name. Point to the third column and explain that **things** also have different names. Ask students to imagine that all the objects in the room have the same name: *blip.* Hold up an eraser, a marking pen, scissors, etc., and explain that each of these is called a blip. Ask students what might happen if you were to ask them to bring you a blip. Summarize by suggesting that there are very good reasons why we have different names for people, places, and things.

 THROUGH

Tell students that Wordy has a very good question for them in this lesson's poem. Wordy's question has to do with how things get their names. Ask students to listen to find out what Wordy wants to know. Read the poem aloud several times.

> **Who Thinks Up Names?**
>
> Who thinks up all the names for things—
>   Like pencil, paper, desk, and book,
> And airplane, bus, and ten-speed bike?
>   Wow! Think of all the time it took!
>
> Who thinks up all the names for places—
>   Stores and cities, rivers, too?
> Who thinks up names for schools and streets?
>   I know it wasn't me or you!
>
> Who thinks up all the names for people,
>   So they won't all be the same?
> At least I know who named me **Wordy**.
>   Thank you, Papa, for my name!

Discuss Wordy's question and how people, places, and things get their names. Ask students if they know who gave them their own names.

Distribute copies of Blackline Master 12. Ask students to follow along, join in, and identify key words as you guide them through several choral readings.

Discuss Wordy Birdy's actions in the illustration next to the poem. Ask students to decide in which column on the board each of the names that Wordy is looking at should be placed. Have students find and read aloud Wordy's talk bubble: *"Your turn! Be sure to name the things in your pictures!"* Call attention to the empty boxes and the place for names under each box. Explain that students are to draw a *person*, a *place*, and a *thing* and write the naming word for each picture. Tell students that special names need to begin with a capital letter. Provide the opportunity for students to complete the activity on their own.

> Wordy Birdy knows that months and days of the week have names, and that their names, like his, begin with a capital letter. He can spell them using My Spell Check. See page 87. (Order form, last page.)

 BEYOND

This activity focuses on the recognition of nouns. You will have many opportunities to reinforce the concept of "naming things" through daily experiences with language. Here are a few possibilities:

1. **Find the Names:** Write the following short paragraph on the board, on a chart, or on a worksheet:

    A little black dog came to our school. The dog was very hot and tired. The dog wanted to come in but the principal said, "You can't come in, because you are a hot dog."

Have students underline the words that name things and talk about the joke in the story.

2. **All About Me:** Have students write a short
   autobiography that uses the following
   sentence frames. These frames may be put
   on the board or a worksheet.

   My name is _____.

   I live at _____ in
   _____.

   I go to _____ School.

   My teacher's name is _____.

3. **Big or Little?** For students needing additional
   instruction on the use of capital letters for
   proper nouns, put a series of words similar to
   the following on the board: *pizza, cream, june,
   michael jordan, bird, mrs. green, three little pigs,
   wordy birdy,* etc. Ask students to identify special
   names of people, places, or things that need
   capital letters.

LESSON 13
Verbs:
Funny Bunny, Fat Cat

 INTO

Introduce or reinforce the concept of words
that tell what things do (verbs) by asking a
volunteer to come to the front of the class.

Explain that the volunteer is going to do what
you whisper in her/his ear and that the class will
have to guess what that action is. After you
whisper actions such as **jump**, **hop**, **sing**, **count**,
yell, etc., write about the action in a short
sentence that students dictate: **Jimmy can jump**;
Suzy can yell; etc. Remind students that they
have already learned about words that name
things. Now they're going to have fun with words
that tell what people and things do. Sometimes
these words are called action words; sometimes
they are called verbs. These are good words to
know when students are writing. Ask students to
generate a list of action words that can be written
on the board or on a chart. For reinforcement, ask
a student to point to a word on the list and have
the class act out that word.

THROUGH

Tell students that in this poem Wordy Birdy
meets two animals that are doing many things.
Have students listen to find out what the animals
do. Read the poem aloud several times. Have
students identify, discuss, and act out the actions
of the bunny and the cat. Ask students which
animal they think Wordy likes the best. Why?

Funny Bunny, Fat Cat

Funny Bunny!

Jump, run,

 Hide, hop,

Sniff, chew,

 Never stop.

Funny Bunny!

Fat Cat!

Chase, claw,

 Scratch, hiss,

Race, meow,

 Jump, miss.

Fat Cat!

Distribute copies of Blackline Master 13. Have students follow along, join in, and identify key words as you guide them through several choral readings.

Call attention to the illustrations next to the poem. Ask students to identify action words that tell what is happening. Focus on Wordy's talk bubble that says: *"Your turn! Write the words that tell what **I** can do and the words that tell what **you** can do."* Read the list of words in the middle of the page *(sing, fly, play)*. Have students put the words in the appropriate list(s).

 **BEYOND**

As your students expand their writing abilities, a visual chart of action words may be a helpful resource. The following activities provide practice with action words:

1. **Show-Me Sentence Strips:** Prepare five or six simple sentence-strip questions on oak tag similar to the following: *Can you hop? Show me. Can you jump? Show me. Can you sing? Show me.* Students can use the sentence strips with a partner, a small group, the whole class, or at a learning center.

2. **I Can:** Label a gallon can with the words **I can**. Ask students to draw pictures of things they can do *(skate, ride a bike, tie shoelaces, bake cookies, read a book)* on 3" x 3" pieces of construction paper. Have students write the action word or words on the back of each picture before placing the picture in the can. You will pick pictures from the can and call on students to try to identify the action using the picture before verifying with the action word or words on the back.

3. **Lots of Action:** Using a big book selection, a chart story, or a familiar chant or poem on the overhead, have students volunteer to frame an action word in context. Discuss the meaning of the word and see if students can think of other words to substitute.

LESSON 14

Adjectives:

I Saw . . .

 INTO

Introduce or reinforce the concept of words that tell about people, places, or things (adjectives) by writing the following sentence on the board or overhead: **Wordy Birdy ate a worm.** Read the sentence aloud with students. Explain that words paint a picture in our heads as we read. Ask them to imagine what the scene looks like as they read the sentence. Prompt students to contribute words that describe by asking: How did Wordy look? Why did he eat the worm? What did the worm look like? As students respond, add descriptive words to the sentence on the board: **A hungry, yellow Wordy Birdy ate a big, fat, squiggly worm.** Have students compare the final sentence with the original: Which sentence helps you see a clearer picture of Wordy and the worm?

Tell students that all writers try to think of different words that tell about people, places, or things. The words that students use in their writing will help make a good picture for readers.

 **THROUGH**

Tell students that Wordy Birdy has written a poem about an adventure with a cat. Wordy adds more and more words to his poem so that you can get the picture. Listen to find out how Wordy wrote the poem and why the ending is funny. Read the poem aloud several times.

> **I Saw . . .**
>
> I saw a cat.
>
> I saw a big cat.
>
> I saw a big, white cat.
>
> I saw a big, white, hissing cat.
>
> I saw a big, white, hissing cat chasing.
>
> I saw a big, white, hissing cat chasing me.
>
> **I'm out of here!**

Discuss how Wordy's description got better and better. Discuss the funny ending. Tell students that they will see how Wordy's poem grew and grew when they get their own copy.

Distribute copies of Blackline Master 14. Have students follow along, join in, and identify key words as you guide them through several choral readings.

Call attention to the cartoon story in the middle of the page. Have students describe the action in each of the pictures. Have students find a sentence from the poem that matches each of the pictures. Find Wordy's talk bubble in the middle of the page. Read his request: *"Your turn! Make a poem like mine that tells about something."* Ask students how these sentence frames look like Wordy's poem. Discuss how Wordy added a new word or words to each line of his poem about the cat. Tell students that they can pick anything or anybody to write a poem about. Have students generate some possible nouns for their poems *(car, snowman, bike, pizza, etc.).* Model the development of one such poem on the board. Provide time for students to complete and share their poems.

 **BEYOND**

This activity offers one introduction to the use of adjectives in students' writing. The following experiences reinforce that concept:

1. **Brainstorming Picture Words:** Write any concrete noun on the board or overhead. Draw a circle around the word. Have five or six lines radiating from the circle. Ask students to give you words that describe the noun and write these words on the spokes. As students are able, divide them into collaborative groups to do this same activity on their own with new nouns they encounter.

2. **Describing Animals:** As part of a unit on animal study or as a follow-up to an appropriate selection about animals, have students select one animal and draw a colorful picture of this animal in its habitat. Students can then exchange pictures and describe, either orally or in writing, what they see. Tell them to use as many descriptive words as they can.

3. **From Pictures to Print:** Have students search through magazines for interesting pictures that call for descriptive language. Students can paste their picture on construction paper and dictate or write a descriptive sentence that captures the sense of the picture.

> Wordy Birdy gets more practice stretching sentences in Stretch It, a feature in every unit in the Spelling Sourcebook Series.

24

LESSON 15
Following Directions:
Wordy Birdy, Wordy Birdy

INTO

Poor Wordy! His world is filled with directions coming from everywhere and everyone: **STOP! GO! SIT! STAND! DRAW! WRITE! FIND! WAIT! READ!** Your students will empathize with Wordy's dilemma since they too may be overwhelmed with the language and concepts involved in following directions. This is especially true in written directions. Yet your students will be required to read directions carefully with understanding many times during the coming years. This lesson's poem provides a whimsical review of following directions as Wordy struggles through this version of the Teddy Bear jump-rope rhyme.

Introduce the lesson by asking students if they are familiar with the Teddy Bear jump-rope rhyme. Chant the rhyme in a chorus several times:

> Teddy Bear, Teddy Bear, turn around;
> Teddy Bear, Teddy Bear, touch the ground;
> Teddy Bear, Teddy Bear, count to three;
> Teddy Bear, Teddy Bear, touch your knee.

Explain that the chant is asking Teddy Bear to follow directions. Write on the board: **Follow the directions.** Discuss some times when following directions is very important: driving a car; baking a cake; fire drills; putting a bike together; etc. Ask students to pretend that they are Teddy Bear and as you read the rhyme once again, have students follow the directions.

THROUGH

Tell students that Wordy has borrowed the Teddy Bear rhyme for today's poem. Wordy has done this because people are always asking him to *follow the directions* and he wants to learn to listen more carefully. Ask students to pretend that they are showing Wordy Birdy how to follow the directions in the poem. As you read the poem aloud several times, have students pantomime the actions.

> **Wordy Birdy, Wordy Birdy**
> Wordy Birdy, Wordy Birdy, turn around.
> Wordy Birdy, Wordy Birdy, touch the ground.
> Wordy Birdy, Wordy Birdy, count to three.
> Wordy Birdy, Wordy Birdy, touch your knee.

Distribute copies of Blackline Master 15. Have students follow along, join in, and identify key words as you guide them through several choral readings. Ask students to identify which words are the action words that tell Wordy what to do.

Call attention to Wordy Birdy's action in the illustration next to the poem. Have students identify which direction in the poem Wordy is following.

Read aloud the message in Wordy's talk bubble: *"Your turn! Follow the directions!"* Have students read the directions under each of the four boxes on the page. Have students work independently, with a partner, or in a guided group to complete the page.

BEYOND

Each hour of the teaching day provides many opportunities to reinforce the concept of following directions. However, many students will need additional practice in listening and reading carefully. Here are a few possibilities:

1. **Wordy Birdy Says:** Instead of "Simon Says," play "Wordy Birdy Says" as reinforcement for listening carefully to oral directions. Encourage volunteers to become "Wordy Birdy" and to lead this popular game.

2. **Read-and-Do:** Use oak-tag strips to prepare five or six simple sentences that give directions: *Go to the door; Stand up and jump; Put your thumb on your nose;* etc. Do some silent teaching. At appropriate times, hold up a sentence strip and see how quickly students can read it silently and follow directions.

3. **Say It Back:** After you have given directions to students for any activity, ask one or two students to paraphrase the directions. This lets you know that your directions were understood and that students are listening carefully. Those students who were able to paraphrase accurately can become your "short" teachers; they can serve as a resource to clarify assignments for other students, freeing you for other tasks.

LESSON 16
Punctuation:
Macaroni #2

 INTO

Your students may have already been introduced to punctuation marks as you developed concepts of print through chorally reading charts and big books. In their writing,

however, some students may be confused regarding the use of a period or question mark. Students learned about Wordy's favorite food, macaroni, in Lesson 11. This rhyme extends the same poem, adding questions and answers.

Place the following statements and questions on the board *without* punctuation: **Can you jump/I can jump; Are you six/I am seven; Who is your friend/You are my friend**. Call students' attention to the missing punctuation marks. Explain that without periods or question marks, it is harder to tell if the sentence is an asking one or a telling one. Ask students to read aloud the first pair and decide which sentence gets a period and which gets a question mark. Have a volunteer fill in the punctuation. Do the same with the other pairs of sentences.

Introduce students to Puppet Master 2, **Queenie Question Mark**, and Puppet Master 3, **Polly Period**. Explain that these puppets have come to help students know which punctuation mark to put at the end of sentences. Say simple questions and statements as students point to the appropriate punctuation mark.

THROUGH

Tell students that Wordy has something old and something new in this lesson's rhyme. Ask students to listen to discover what is old and what is new. Read the poem aloud several times.

> **Macaroni #2**
> Macaroni, macaroni,
> That's the stuff for me.
> Macaroni, macaroni,
> Messy as can be.
>
> Do I have it on my jeans?
> Yes, you have it on your jeans!
>
> Do I have it on my shirt?
> Yes, you have it on your shirt!
>
> Do I have it on my shoes?
> Yes, you have it on your shoes!

Wordy Birdy can write more verses using words from his My Spell Check (see page 87): "Do I have it on my <u>jacket</u>? Yes, you have it on your jacket! Do I have it on my <u>yellow boots</u>? Yes, you have it on your yellow boots!"

Have students follow along, join in, and identify key words as you guide them through several choral readings. Students will recognize Wordy's favorite food, macaroni, from an earlier lesson. Discuss the new questions and answers at the end of the poem.

Distribute copies of Blackline Master 16. Have students point to their *jeans, shirts,* and *shoes* when those parts of the poem are read. On successive readings, have half the students ask the questions as the others respond with the answers.

Ask students to describe what is taking place in the illustration.

Focus attention on Wordy's request that asks students to put *Queenie* and *Polly* in the right place. Have students complete the questions and answers, putting in the correct punctuation.

BEYOND

As students grow in competence and confidence, their writing will reflect appropriate punctuation. The following activities may reinforce their understanding:

1. **Queenie Question Mark:** Begin a chart that has a picture of **Queenie Question Mark** at the top (See Puppet Master 2). Under Queenie's picture write: *Words that Ask Questions.* As new "question words" are encountered, add them to the chart which will include words such as: *who, what, where, when, why, can, do,* etc.

2. **On Your Mark:** Prepare punctuation-mark popsicle sticks or have children make their own sets. Cut out and paste two round circles

of construction paper at the top of two popsicle sticks. Have students draw a question mark on one and a period on the other. Call out a question or statement. Students will hold up the appropriate punctuation popsicle stick. Encourage students to make up their own questions and statements for one another.

3. **Fix-It-Up:** Put a short paragraph of high interest on the board or on a worksheet. Do **NOT** include punctuation; have students add the punctuation.

LESSON 17
Compound Words:
Two Words in One

INTO

Explain that Wordy Birdy has a new trick to show students about some words they will meet in their reading and writing. Write **cow** and **boy** on the board. Ask students what each of these words means. Explain that sometimes two words can join together to make a new word that means something different. Write **cowboy** on the board and discuss its meaning. Demonstrate compound words using several examples: *out side; every thing; dog house.* Discuss the meanings of these words separately and in their compound form.

THROUGH

Introduce *Two Words in One* by showing Blackline Master 17 and asking students what Wordy is doing on the poem page. (He is stretching words apart or putting words together.) Explain that Wordy Birdy's rhyme for this lesson has to do with putting two words together to make a compound word. Ask them to listen for words that can go together or be split apart. Read the poem aloud several times. Ask students to identify the compound words they hear.

> **Two Words in One**
>
> Football, snowman, cowgirls, too,
> Look at what these words can do!
> They go together for a start,
> Or we can take these words apart!

Distribute copies of Blackline Master 17. Have students follow along, join in, and identify key words as you guide them through several choral readings. Ask students to take apart the compound words and discuss their meanings separately and together.

Call attention to Wordy Birdy's actions in the illustration. Discuss the compound word Wordy is holding. Read through the lists of words at the bottom of the page. Ask students to first connect the parts of each compound word with their pointer finger before they draw the line and write the word. Ask students to use the compound word in a sentence. Encourage students to keep an eye out for any new compound words they encounter in their reading.

 BEYOND

This rhyme can serve as an introduction to recognizing compound words. The lesson may also be used for practice, reinforcement, or evaluation. For additional practice, try the following:

1. **Everybody Show:** Have students make "Everybody Show" holders by folding an 8½" x 3½" piece of construction paper ½ inch from the bottom and stapling the edges. Distribute three or four small (3" x 3") word cards to each student. Each card will have a simple word that makes up the second half of a compound and students will have different words on their cards. As you hold up the first half of a compound, students search for an appropriate second half, place it in their holder, then hold up their holder. Not all students will be able to match each word.

2. **Draw It Out:** Have students fold a piece of drawing paper into four sections. Divide the class in half. Without the other half being able to hear, show one half of the class the four words that they will illustrate in their boxes: *ball, man, yard, bell.* Go over each word before students begin to draw. Without the first half being able to hear, show the remaining half of the class the four words that they will illustrate in their boxes: *snowball, Spiderman, farmyard, doorbell.* Go over each word before students begin to draw. When completed, have students from each half pair up to discuss their drawings. Emphasize that the meaning of the word changes when it becomes a compound.

3. **Secrets!** Give each student a 3" x 3" piece of construction paper with a "secret" compound word written on it. Check to see that students understand their secret word. Have students illustrate their word on the other side of the paper. In groups of four or five, have students share their drawings so that others can guess which compound word they have illustrated. If no one is able to guess, the illustrator can give clues.

Wordy Birdy can find compound words such as grandma, grandpa, classroom, playground, and hamburger on My Spell Check (see page 87).

28

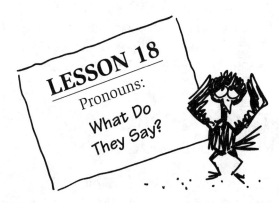

LESSON 18
Pronouns:
What Do
They Say?

 INTO

Pronouns are often confusing to young children, especially when they refer to a previously mentioned individual or individuals. This lesson's rhyme, *What Do They Say?*, can be a useful introduction or reinforcement for working with pronouns.

Say, "I am Mrs./Ms./Mr. _____. I am a teacher." Explain that if one of the students was telling someone about you, they couldn't say "I am Mrs./Ms./Mr. _____." Ask students how they would change the words. Write: **My teacher is Mrs./Ms./Mr. _____. She/He is my teacher.** Ask students who the word *she/he* is talking about. Replace *she/he* with the opposite gender pronoun. Ask students why that isn't right. Make two columns on the board: *Girls* and *Boys*. Hold up the word cards **he, she, his, hers, him, her, me, I**. Have students determine which column or columns the pronouns belong in. Hold up **it** and discuss what this word might describe. Make a new column for **it**. Hold up and discuss **they, their, them, ours**, etc.

 **THROUGH**

Tell students that Wordy Birdy is confused. He can't figure out the right word to use. Ask students to listen to the poem to find out why Wordy is having trouble. Read the poem aloud several times. Ask students to identify words that are a problem to Wordy.

What Do They Say?

HE'S a HE; HE'S not a WE,
And SHE is not an IT.
And sometimes I am only ME.
When does the right word fit?
I know that WE are not a THEM,
And THEM is sometimes THEY,
But how 'bout YOU and HER and HIM?
Who knows what's right to say?

Ask students to point to themselves or one another as you call out: **he, her, me, I, you**, etc.

Distribute copies of Blackline Master 18. Have students identify key words as you guide them through several choral readings.

Call attention to Wordy Birdy's action in the illustration next to the poem. Ask students to describe what is wrong with Wordy's labels over the girl and boy. Read aloud what Wordy Birdy is saying in the middle of the page: *"Your turn! Make some pictures that match."* Call attention to the labels in the empty boxes. Read the labels aloud with students. Discuss the kinds of pictures they could draw for each box.

Wordy Birdy can find all the pronouns in this lesson on My Spell Check (see page 87).

 **BEYOND**

There will be many opportunities throughout the school year to focus on pronouns. The following activities may prove useful:

1. *Our Own Labels:* Arrange cards with the following words along a board ledge: **he, she, them, they, her, his, him, we, you**. Ask a group of students to come to the board. Select a volunteer to "label" students by handing an appropriate card to individuals or clusters. Ask the rest of the students if they are in

agreement with the choices. Choose other students to be the person labeling the individuals and groups.

2. **Fill-In Fun:** Write the following sentence frames on the board or overhead. Ask students to place the appropriate pronouns in the missing spaces. They may do this orally or in writing.

_____ has a little brother.

_____ has to take care of _____ little brother.

_____ is a messy eater.

_____ has to wash _____ after lunch.

Similar sentences can be presented orally or on simple worksheets to be completed and illustrated.

3. **Stand Up, Sit Down:** Using Wordy Birdy's rhyme, have students actively respond to the poem by standing when they hear a pronoun that applies to them. Repeat the activity with students responding to word cards.

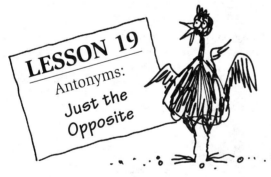

LESSON 19
Antonyms:
Just the Opposite

 INTO

An effective way to introduce the concept of opposites, or antonyms, involves movement. Make four hand-held "traffic" signs: **STOP**, **GO**, **FAST**, **SLOW**. Introduce the signs and the meaning of their commands to students. As students get into a jogging, hopping, skipping, or jumping movement, hold up each command sign, one at a time. Praise students for their ability to follow

directions! When students are seated, hold a discussion on the responses to each sign. Ask students to explain the difference between STOP and GO, FAST and SLOW. Explain that when words are very different they are the *opposite.* Ask students if they know any opposites words.

 THROUGH

Tell students that Wordy Birdy has just discovered what *opposite* means. Wordy has written a special *Just the Opposite* rhyme. Ask students to listen for the special joke at the end of the rhyme. Read the poem aloud several times and discuss the meaning of the ending.

> **Just the Opposite**
> Wordy says **yes**. You say **no**!
> Wordy says **stop**. You say **go**!
> Wordy says **fast**. You say **slow**!
> Wordy says fly. You say NO WAY!

Distribute copies of Blackline Master 19. Encourage students to follow along, join in, and identify key words as you guide them through several choral readings. This is an ideal selection for discussing punctuation and the difference between periods and exclamation points.

Call attention to the actions in the illustration. Have two students act out the picture in the illustration. Then call attention to Wordy saying: *"Your turn! I'll say the word and you say the opposite."* Take students through the paired sentences, asking for their responses. Have students explain how they were able to figure out an opposite word. Tell students that opposite words may also be called *antonyms*.

> Wordy Birdy likes to play an "opposite game" with My Spell Check (see page 87). He writes words he finds on My Spell Check that have an opposite, then he writes their antonym partner.

BEYOND

This lesson is an effective lead-in to further work with antonyms in your curriculum. For additional practice, try the following:

1. **Match Up:** Write pairs of familiar opposites on cards, one word per card. Distribute the word cards to students. Each student should get one-half of a pair *(in/out, he/she, boy/girl, above/below, first/last, good/bad, work/play, here/there, off/on, big/little, left/right, large/small)*. After directions are given, have students find their opposite-word partner and read their words to the rest of the class.

2. **Tricky Opposites:** Tell students that they will really need to use their ears and their brains on this movement activity. As you call out a command, students must act out just the opposite. Demonstrate with several tricky commands: *Sit!* (Students must stand.) *Be Quiet!* (Students must talk.) *Hold up your right hand.* (Students must hold up their left hand.) *Face the front of the room.* (Students must face the back of the room.) After you model this activity several times, students can volunteer to be the leader.

3. **Just the Opposite:** Write several simple sentence frames on the board. Students copy the sentences, supplying an opposite word for the underlined words (e.g., *The girl has on a big cap. The man is short. The boy can sit.*)

LESSON 20
Root Words: Watch Them Grow

INTO

Introduce the concept of identifying roots of words, or base words, as one strategy for word recognition by writing an easy and familiar root verb (other than *play*) on the board: **jump**, **walk**, **pick**. *For this introductory lesson, avoid words that change their spelling when adding suffixes.* Ask students if they know that words can grow and change into other words. Relate the concept of growing and changing to the growing process of a plant.

Tell students that Wordy has another way of helping them figure out new words. Turn to the familiar word on the board, explaining that ____ is the root of many other words. If they can recognize ____, it will help them figure out the new word made from ____. Ask students if they can think of other words that can grow from ____. Write these words on the board, or demonstrate how ____ can change by adding **-ed**, **-ing**, **-er**, etc. Have students come to the board and frame the root for each word.

THROUGH

Tell students that Wordy has a helping rhyme for figuring out new words. Ask them to listen to see how one of their favorite words can grow. Read the poem aloud several times. Engage students in discussing how the word **play** grew into other words.

> **Watch Them Grow**
>
> Plant a word! It's fun to try.
> You need a verb to start.
> Watch it grow to other words.
> I knew that you were smart!
>
> Let's show you how a word can grow,
> Let's plant a word like **play**.
> It sprouts to **playing**, **played**, **replayed**.
> What others can you say?

Distribute copies of Blackline Master 20. Ask students to follow along, join in, and identify key words as you guide them through several choral readings.

Call attention to Wordy's actions in the illustration. Guide students through finding the root and affixes. Note that the word *player* is not in the poem.

Focus attention on the three words at the bottom of the page. Tell students that it is their turn to do some gardening. Ask for a suggestion as to how each root word might grow. If this is difficult for some students, pair them with others to do some "partner word-gardening."

1. **How Does Your Garden Grow?** Have students create artistic beanstalks by painting or drawing a tall, skinny stalk on their paper. Make a list of common, regularly spelled words on the board, such as *play, call, work, jump, help, look,* etc. Have students select one word, label the **root** of their beanstalk with the word, and create leaves or beans that are labeled with words grown from the root.

2. *Growing Roots that End in "E":* Write the following words on the board: **bike**, **drive**, **share**. Guide students through a mini-lesson demonstrating why **-er**, **-ed**, and **-ing** cannot be added to the word without first throwing away the silent **e** on the end.

3. *See How They Grow:* Provide one third of the class with cards showing easy and familiar root words. Give the other students cards with suffixes: **-er**, **-ed**, **-ing**. Explain that more than one student can be matched to a root. Have students mix and match root words and endings, then share their words with the rest of the class.

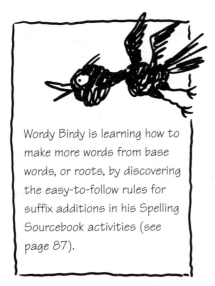

Wordy Birdy is learning how to make more words from base words, or roots, by discovering the easy-to-follow rules for suffix additions in his Spelling Sourcebook activities (see page 87).

 BEYOND

To strengthen the concept that root words can grow and change into other words by adding affixes, try the following activities:

LESSON 21
Plurals:
One Shoe, Two Shoes

INTO

"More than one" is a fairly easy concept for young students. Difficulties arise because of the many different ways our written language has of signifying more than one: **-s**, **-es**, **-ies**, **elf/elves**, **mouse/mice**, **sheep/sheep**. This poem reinforces counting and colors as it introduces the concept of adding **s** to words to signal more than one.

Ask for a volunteer to come to the front of the room. Write on the board above the student's head, **one girl** or **one boy**. Ask three girls or three boys to come to the front of the room. Over their heads write, **three boy** or **three girl** and read the words aloud. Ask students if there is anything funny sounding about saying **three boy** or **three girl**. Ask how they would change the words on the board. Explain that when they are talking or writing about more than one, they add an **s** to the word.

Group familiar objects where students can see them: one paper clip, four paper clips; one marking pen, three marking pens; one pencil, two pencils; etc. Have students raise their hands and describe the groups, as in "I see one *pencil*. I see two *pencils*."

THROUGH

Explain that Wordy Birdy sometimes has problems remembering when to add an **s** to words. That's why he really likes this poem because it helps him to think about adding **s** for more than one. Ask students to listen for familiar counting words, familiar color words, and words that mean more than one. Read the poem aloud several times. Have students point to their one shoe and their two shoes as you read.

> **One Shoe, Two Shoes**
>
> One shoe, two shoes,
> Red shoes, blue shoes,
> > Shoes that slide,
> > Shoes that ride.
>
> One shoe, two shoes,
> White shoes, blue shoes,
> > Shoes that run,
> > Shoes for fun.

Discuss familiar words from the poem: counting words, color words, and words that mean more than one.

Distribute copies of Blackline Master 21. Have students follow along, join in, and identify key words as you guide them through several choral readings.

Ask students to describe Wordy Birdy in the illustration. Can they guess which season of the year it is? Read the labels together. Call attention to Wordy Birdy's talk bubble and read his request aloud. Have students work with a partner to determine which numeral should come in front of each label.

BEYOND

Once students have a clear understanding of the concept of adding **s** to signal more than one, other plural forms can be introduced. Let's start with an easy one:

1. **Sharp Ears:** Have students fold their lined paper in half to make two columns. Demonstrate how to label the headings for each column: **One** and **More than One**. Explain that you will call out words that they know how to spell. If the word means **one**, they write it in that column; if the word means **more than one**, they write it in that column. Dictate words, such as *boys, car, dog, cats, man, she, tables, trees,* etc. Have students buddy with a partner to see if their lists are the same.

2. **Create a Poem:** To help students follow the pattern of *One Shoe, Two Shoes,* put the following poem frame on the board:

    > One ____, two ____,
    > Red ____, blue ____,
    > ____ that ____,
    > ____ that ____.

    Ask students what new words they could use to make up a new poem. List possible suggestions on the board: *flower/flowers, cap/caps, boot/boots, tree/trees, cake/cakes,* etc. Ask students to select one pair for their poem. Remind students that they will have to use words that tell about their special word to finish the poem. Provide opportunities for students to share their poems.

3. **More than One:** To introduce or reinforce the concept of different spellings that signal more than one, draw four columns on the board. Head the first column **one**, the second column **-s**, the third column **-es**, and the fourth column **-ies**. Explain to students that they may have noticed that some words use more than an **s** to signal more than one. Write the word **girl** in column one. Tell students that they already know how to show more than one girl. Ask them what they should put in column two. Now write **dish, box, match, mess** in column one. Explain that some words need more than **s** on the end. Write **dishes, boxes, matches, messes** in column three. Ask students to pronounce these words. Ask students why they think these words need **-es** at the end. Write **pony, puppy, baby** in column one. Ask students what is the same about the spelling of these three words. (They end in consonant-**y**.) Explain that when a word ends in consonant-**y**, the **y** often changes to **ies** to show more than one. Ask students to spell the plurals as you write them in column four. This chart would make an effective reference for students.

LESSON 22
Multiple Meanings: Tricky Words

INTO

To introduce or reinforce the concept of words that have multiple meanings, write the following sentence frames on the board:

I sneeze when I have a _____.

It's too _____ to go swimming.

Prepare a word card labeled **cold**. Using the Wordy Birdy puppet, explain that Wordy is having a confusing day. Just when he thinks he knows what a new word means, he finds out that the same word also means something else! What's a bird to do?

Hold up the word card **cold** and explain that **cold** is one of the words confusing Wordy. Ask students to tell you what the word means by putting it to work in a sentence. Encourage different usages of the word. Draw attention to the sentences on the board. Read each sentence aloud and have a volunteer place the word card in the appropriate space. Emphasize the different meanings of **cold**.

 THROUGH

Explain to students that they will find many tricky words that look and sound the same but mean different things. Ask students to listen to see if they can figure out the two tricky words in

Wordy's poem. Read the poem aloud several times. Engage students in discussing the different meanings of **lap** and **can.**

Tricky Words

A kitty can lap some milk,

And I can lap a mile,

But sitting on my mama's lap

Can really make me smile!

My daddy cans some peaches,

And I can can some, too.

We can them in a gallon can,

It's really fun to do.

Distribute copies of Blackline Master 22. Have students follow along, join in, and identify key words as you guide them through several choral readings.

Call attention to Wordy Birdy's actions in the two illustrations. Have students point to the appropriate picture as you read the sentence. Then have students point again to the picture where **lap** means a place to sit and where **lap** means going around a track. Ask if **lap** can mean anything else (waves lapping on the beach; dogs/cats lapping water or milk).

Call attention to Wordy Birdy's talk bubble and the sentence frames below the title **Run.** Read the directions with students: *"Your turn! The word is spelled the same but the meaning is different! Write the word **run** in each blank space."* To check prior knowledge, ask students to explain what this word means by giving examples. Engage students in choral reading of the sentence frames. Then have them write **run** on all three blanks. Provide time for students to share their sentences orally.

BEYOND

This rhyme is a natural lead-in to reinforce multiple-meaning words, as well as words that take the form of both nouns and verbs (planted a plant, fishing for fish, etc.). Some additional activities might include:

1. **Mix and Match:** Put the following pairs of sentences on the board in two columns. Distribute 3" x 3" squares of construction paper. Half of your students will illustrate the sentences in column A; the other half will illustrate those in column B. Have students first find the matching partner for **bark,** then hold up their pictures and explain the two different meanings. Do the same with **water** and **park.**

Column A	Column B
A dog can **bark.**	A tree has **bark.**
I want a drink of **water.**	We need to **water** the plants.
My sister can **park** a car.	We can play in the **park.**

2. **Tricky Words Chart:** Start a chart of familiar words with more than one meaning. Have students illustrate the different meanings on 3" x 3" squares of construction paper that can be placed by the word on the chart.

3. **Tricky Words Book:** Start a class book by passing out pieces of construction paper which students fold in half. Students pull a multiple-meaning word from a hat, draw two illustrations (one on each half) representing different meanings of the word. If possible, write or dictate two simple sentences using the two different meanings. Possible words might include: *ride, cut, down, feet, hard, help, line,* etc.

Can Word Birdy's friends find the words that Wordy saw on My Spell Check that have more than one meaning? (See page 87.)

LESSON 23
Synonyms:
Say It Better

 **INTO**

Introduce the concept of synonyms to your students by writing **big boy** on the board or overhead. Tell students that you want to write a story about a boy but you are discouraged because **big** just doesn't tell how really big this boy is. Shake your head as you erase **big** and pretend to throw the word in the wastebasket. Ask students to help you think of a word that isn't as ordinary as **big**. Write their suggestions in a list in front of **boy**. Encourage words like **enormous**, **gigantic**, **huge**, etc. Show your pleasure as you compliment students on their help.

 **THROUGH**

Announce that Wordy Birdy is having the very same problem today: trying to think of words that are new and exciting instead of words that are used and old. Ask students to listen for words that are old and words that are new in his poem. Read the poem aloud several times. Discuss the different words used in the poem.

Say It Better

Some words are old. Put them away!
Let's use some other words today.

Instead of **big**, say **huge** or **wide**.
Instead of **said**, think **shouted**, **cried**.

Instead of **little**, why not **tiny**?
Pick words that sparkle, new and shiny!

Discuss the different words used in the poem. Distribute copies of Blackline Master 23. Have students follow along, join in, and identify key words as you guide them through several choral readings.

Call attention to Wordy Birdy's actions. Ask why he is holding up **huge** and **tiny** instead of **big** and **little**. Ask students to suggest other words that can be used in place of **big** and **little**.

Have students find Wordy's talk bubble. Read his request. Go over the example of changing **little** to **small**. Ask for other possibilities (*tiny*, *teeny*, *eensy*, etc.). Have students work with a study buddy to find new words for **bad**, **walked**, **good**, and **tall**. Provide the opportunity for students to share their words.

 **BEYOND**

This lesson encourages students to select descriptive language that is vivid; to move beyond the ordinary and use their expanding vocabulary. The poem can provide a meaningful pre-writing experience. Use the following activities for additional practice:

1. **Painting Word Pictures:** Write the following sentence on the chalkboard: **The dog barked.** Ask students to close their eyes and imagine that they can see the dog. Have students open their eyes and discuss their *mind pictures.* Emphasize the differences in their descriptions. Explain that by adding some words, we can get another picture of the dog. Ask students to contribute words that describe the dog (size, color, breed, etc.). Add their responses to the sentence. Now ask students to close their eyes and get a new picture of the more detailed sentence. Encourage them to use vivid language in their own descriptions.

2. **Say-It-Better Story Frame:** Put the following story frame on a worksheet.

    Once upon a time there was a ____ girl who was on her way to see her ____

Granny. She was ____ in the ____ woods when, all of a sudden, out jumped a ____ wolf. "Oh," she ____, "please don't eat me!" And she threw her ____ basket of food and soda at the ____ wolf. The cans of soda hit the wolf on the head and knocked him out. The ____ girl put the food and soda back in the basket and went to Granny's.

After going over the story several times with students, have them work with a partner to fill in some new words. Encourage them to use approximate spellings—to use letters that match the sounds they hear in the words. Have students share their versions.

3. **Mix-and-Match:** Prepare sets of simple synonyms with one word to a card *(little/ small/tiny, said/yelled/shouted, friend/buddy, airplane/jet, etc.).* Pass out the cards. At your signal, students search for and find word cards that mean the same. Have students share their matches.

LESSON 24
Contractions:
Taking Shortcuts

 INTO

Introduce the concept of contractions to your students with **Appy Apostrophe**, Puppet Master 4. Explain that Appy loves to take shortcuts. To check students' understanding of the word short-cuts, ask students to tell about shortcuts they have taken. Explain that Appy takes shortcuts by squishing two words together and leaving one or more letters out of the new word he makes. These

words are called contractions. Show them how Appy always hops into words in place of the missing letters to signal a contraction shortcut. Demonstrate with some examples on the board: **I am** becomes **I'm**; **you will** becomes **you'll**.

 THROUGH

Explain that in today's Wordy Birdy rhyme, Wordy wants the boys and girls to join him in some contraction shortcuts. Ask students to listen for shortcut words. Read the poem aloud several times. Ask students to identify the shortcut contraction words that need **Appy Apostrophe**.

> **Taking Shortcuts**
>
> You say **do not**. I say **don't**.
>
> You say **will not**. I say **won't**.
>
> Which is quicker? Which is fast?
>
> Take a shortcut—don't be last!

Distribute copies of Blackline Master 24. Have students follow along, join in, and identify key words as you guide them through several choral readings.

Call attention to Wordy Birdy's action in the illustration. What is Wordy doing? Why?

Read Wordy Birdy's directions in the talk bubble. Explain that Wordy wants students to make new shortcut words that use **Appy Apostrophe**. As students suggest possibilities for shortening **it is** in the first example, write their responses on the board. Explain why **it's** is the correct new word by showing that Appy takes the place of the **i** in **is**. Read the whole sentence aloud. Follow the same process for the other three examples.

 BEYOND

There will be many opportunities to practice using contractions in student writing.

37

The following activities provide reinforcement:

1. **I Will, I Won't:** Ask students to fold their paper into two halves. At the top of one half, have students draw a smiling face with the word **I'll**; at the top of the other half, have them draw a frowning face with the words **I won't**. Ask students to draw or write about things that they **will** or **won't** do in the appropriate column. For example: *I'll swim in the sea; I won't eat raw fish.* Have them share their papers. The same activity can be done to practice **I can/I can't**; **I do/I don't**; **I would/I wouldn't**.

2. **Mix and Match:** Give half of the students cards with non-contracted versions of words; give the other half cards with the contracted versions of the words. Have students find their partner. Ask each pair of students to look carefully at their words and explain to the class which letters stay and which letters are replaced with an apostrophe.

3. **Using Contractions:** Ask students to select one of the four activity statements on Wordy Birdy Blackline Master 24. The sentence they select will become the lead (topic) sentence for a short paragraph they will write that tells more about the statement. Tell students to use two contractions that are familiar.

Wordy Birdy and his buddies like to play a game using their My Spell Check cards (see page 87). They use My Spell Check to name words that the others must use to form a contraction.

LESSON 25
Double Letters:
Can You Find Me?

 INTO

Write the following words on the board: **funny, mess, street, spell, moon.** Point to each word and say the word aloud, having students say it aloud with you. Ask students what is alike about the spelling of these words. *(They contain double letters.)* Underline the double letters in each word as you and your students read it aloud. Note that double letters represent one sound. Ask students to look around the *room* to see if they can find other words or object names that have double letters *(wall, floor, books, penny)*. Write their words on the board so they can see that the words contain double letters.

 **THROUGH**

Tell students Wordy has a mystery and needs their help. Ask them to listen and try to find the answer to the riddle in the poem. Read the poem aloud several times. Ask students if they have an answer for Wordy. *(Some of the words contain double letters.)*

> **Can You Find Me?**
>
> Can you find me?
> I'm easy to see.
> I'm in wiggle and giggle,
> And bee and tree.
>
> I'm in look and book,
> And little and fiddle.
> If I'm not at the end,
> I'll be in the middle.

Distribute copies of Blackline Master 25. Have students follow along, join in, and identify words that contain double letters as you guide them through several choral readings.

Call attention to Wordy Birdy's actions in the illustration next to the poem. Ask students to describe what Wordy is doing and why. Ask students what is alike about the two words. What are the double letters in **little** called? *(consonants)* What are the double letters in **look** called? *(vowels)* Have students find the talk bubble where Wordy says: *"Your turn! Use these double letters to spell the words in my poem."* Read the poem aloud with students furnishing the missing double letters. Then have students write the missing double letters in the incomplete words. Encourage students to share their completed poem with a buddy.

> Wordy Birdy likes the big Teaching Poster and his own Personal Poster in the Level 1 Spelling Sourcebook that correlate with this lesson. (Spelling Sourcebook Teaching Poster sets can be purchased separately. See page 87.)

 BEYOND

This lesson offers an introduction to and/or reinforcement of the spelling of double-letter words. These activities provide more practice:

1. **Make-A-Word:** Using oak tag or construction paper, write a different familiar double-letter word on a card for each student. Leave enough space between each of the letters so they can be cut apart. Distribute a word and an envelope to each student. Demonstrate how students can cut the word apart, letter-by-letter, and put the letters into their envelope. Have students trade envelopes, arrange the letters to make a word, and copy the word on the front of the envelope. Students can continue to use these envelopes for practice at a learning center.

2. **"Who Am I?" Poems:** Write the following poem frames on the board or overhead. List the following letter combinations on the board: **bb, tt, ll, oo, ee.** Tell students that the same letter combination will be used for all four words in poem number 1. Ask students to try each combination in the words and raise their hand when they have a combination that fits. Have students fill in the missing letters. Do the same with poem 2. Once the poems are complete, invite students to join in a choral reading of the poems.

    1. Who am I?
        You'll find me twice
        In le_ _ er and be_ _ er
        And in ba_ _ er and ma_ _ er,
        But not in mice.

    2. Who am I?
        You'll find me twice
        In sch_ _l and p_ _l
        And in c_ _l and t_ _l,
        But not in mice.

3. **Mix-And-Match:** Use the two *Who Am I?* poems. Ask students to number the double-letter words in the poems from 1–8 (four words in each poem). Have students count off by numbers 1 through 8. Students will make a word card with the double-letter word that matches their number. When students have written the word on their card, ask them to find a rhyming match. Pairs of students will then say their words and identify the double-letter match.

> Wordy Birdy challenges students to find every double-letter word on My Spell Check! Then sort the words by the letters that are doubled. (See page 87.)

LESSON 26
Consonant Blends:
Wordy's Blending Sounds Today

INTO

We suggest you bring an actual blender to class for this introduction of initial consonant blends. Using several available fruits or fruit juices, show students how a blender operates. Explain that it mixes things together, but that you can still taste some of the original fruit. Students will probably have had their own experiences with milk-shake blenders or with yogurt machines that blend flavors. Tell students that they can blend letters in words without a machine. Write some simple words with initial consonant blends: **black**, **brown**, **green**, **blue**. Students should quickly recognize these familiar color words. Ask students to listen carefully as you pronounce the beginning of each word. Explain that the letters blend together but that you can still hear the sound of each letter just as you can taste strawberries and bananas mixed together in a blender.

Have students look around the room and identify an object by saying the name of the object. Then have them tell whether or not they hear two sounds blended together at the beginning of the word. When students identify a word that begins with a blend, write it on the board and have students say it aloud with you (e.g., *flag, clock, floor, blinds*, etc.).

THROUGH

Tell students that Wordy has been having some fun blending sounds today and ask students to listen carefully for the blended sounds in each

of Wordy's words. Read the poem several times, encouraging students to join in.

> **Wordy's Blending Sounds Today**
>
> Wordy's blending sounds today;
> He says it's fun to do.
>
> Wordy's blending sounds today;
> He has some words for you.
>
> **Fl**ee, **fl**y, **fl**ew;
>   **Bl**ack, **bl**ond, **bl**ue;
> **Gr**een, **gr**ow, **gr**ew;
>   **St**op, **st**amp, **st**ew.

Ask students to recall some of Wordy's words and to identify, if possible, the blended sounds. Write student-suggested words on the board, underlining the beginning blends. Ask students what is alike about the words that end each of the last four lines in Wordy's poem. *(They rhyme.)*

Distribute copies of Blackline Master 26. Have students follow along, join in, and identify key words as you guide them through several choral readings.

Call attention to what Wordy is doing in the illustration next to the poem. Have students pronounce the words with you as you emphasize the consonant blend at the beginning of each word.

Find Wordy's talk bubble and have students read aloud with you: *"Your turn! Use the letters to make a new word. Write your new word on the line."* Guide students through completing the activity or, if students are capable, allow students to complete the words on their own. Provide time for students to share their poem aloud.

BEYOND

This lesson offers an introduction to and/or reinforcement of consonant blends. The following activities provide additional practice:

1. **Write a Poem:** Provide students with the following sentence frames and blends on the

board, an overhead, or a worksheet. Have students work with a buddy to write a poem using the consonant blends. Once students have completed their poems, invite one partner to read while the other demonstrates actions for each line of the poem.

fl   sl   cl   dr

The mop goes
(fl) _ _**ip** (fl) _ _**op**.

The water goes
(dr) _ _**ip** (dr) _ _**op**.

The pig goes
(sl) _ _**ip** (sl) _ _**op**.

The horse goes
(cl) _ _**ip** (cl) _ _**op**.

2. **Who/What Am I?** Write the following in a column on the board, on an overhead, or on a worksheet: 1. ___y; 2. ___y; 3. ___own; 4. ___ee; 5. ___op. Above the column, write the consonant blends: **tr**, **cl**, **st**, **cr**, and **fl**. Have students listen carefully for the clues given in each of the following riddles and answer the riddle by writing the appropriate consonant blend on the corresponding line.

Riddles:

1. I buzz around all day. You shoo me away when I try to land on your food. I'm a household pest. What am I? *(fly)*
2. I'm just a baby. I cannot talk. I do this when I'm unhappy or when I want to eat. What do I do? *(cry)*
3. I wear funny clothes and big floppy shoes. I paint my face. I'm a part of the circus. I do silly things to make you laugh. Who am I? *(clown)*
4. You find me outside. I live in the forest. I have roots, branches, and leaves. What am I? *(tree)*
5. I tell you what to do. I'm found on signs on the street. I'm the opposite of **go**. What do I tell you to do? *(stop)*

3. **Mix and Match:** Print or type the following consonant blends and phonograms on a worksheet to be duplicated and distributed. Have students cut out blend and phonogram

squares. Then have students combine blends with phonograms to form words; have them write their new words on lined paper. Provide time for students to orally share and use their new words in sentences. Have students place blend and phonogram squares in an envelope and put it in the reading/writing center for future individual and small-group use. For students who are not ready for so many pieces, create a worksheet with fewer phonograms.

bl	ory	and	ill
st	een	ound	oke
cr	ick	ow	ack
gr	ell	ace	ink
sp	ate	ew	ay

LESSON 27
Words that End in Silent E:
on the End—
A Silent Friend

 INTO

Explain that Wordy Birdy has discovered an important secret about words. Write on the board: **mak, cak, bak**. Ask students what these groups of letters mean. When everyone agrees that these are not words, show them Wordy's secret: add an **e** to the end of each. Ask students if they recognize the words. After they have identified the words, look puzzled as you say, "But the **e** doesn't make a sound." Then turn to Wordy as you say, "Wordy says that's the big secret. **E**'s job is to give us a signal that the **vowel** in the word says its own name." Point to the words on the board. Tell students that **e** is the silent friend in many words. Be sure to clarify that there are also words with **e** on the end that don't fit this pattern. (You may want to deal with exceptions like *come*, *love*, and *done* in another lesson.)

 THROUGH

Tell students that Wordy wants to share his secret of the silent **e** with them. Ask them to listen to Wordy's poem to see if they can answer the question at the end. Read the poem aloud several times.

> **"E" on the End—A Silent Friend**
>
> Tricky little "no sound" **e**
> Sitting on the end.
> Keeping quiet, keeping still,
> What message do you send?

Ask students what message an **e** on the end of a word sends.

Distribute copies of Blackline Master 27. Have students follow along, join in, and identify key words as you guide them through several choral readings.

Call attention to Wordy's actions in the illustration next to the poem. Ask students to describe what Wordy is doing and why he is doing it.

Focus attention on Wordy's talk bubble. Explain that Wordy wants students to add silent **e** to the words so that each question or statement makes sense. Students can complete this activity on their own or with a partner. Then have them read their sentences aloud.

 BEYOND

The following activities offer practice and reinforcement in recognizing words with silent **e**:

1. **Be An "E":** Either write sentences on the board that contain words that end in silent **e** or use a chart or big book that uses these words. Explain to students that everyone will read the passages together as you move your hand under the words. When you come to a word with a silent **e** on the end, students are to put a hand over their mouth. (This may also give you an opportunity to point out the exceptions to the long-vowel-silent-e pattern. Examples include: *come*, *love*, etc.)

2. **Fix It Up:** Put the following paragraph on the board or overhead to do orally. If students are able, put the paragraph on a worksheet that can be completed independently. Explain that students are to use Wordy's secret to fix up some of the words in the story.

   > Help! My house is on fir__. Call 911 for the fir__ department. Tell them I put a cak__ in the stov__ to bak__, and the cak__ caught on fir__.

3. **Everybody Show:** Make simple "Everybody Show" holders by using 8½" x 4" construction paper. Fold up a one-half inch flap and staple at each end. Give each student a silent **e** letter card. Write a list of familiar words on the board: *ride, hid, love, make, cut, face, time, her, done, come, top, hide*, etc. As you read the words together, students will hold up the silent **e** card for those words that follow the cvcv generalization (long-vowel-silent-e pattern).

> Wordy learned in his Spelling Sourcebook activities that a silent *e* at the end of a word is sometimes "sleepy little *e*," as in *little* and *large*. Then he learned that sometimes *e* is "bossy" and makes the vowel say its name, as in *lake* and *like*. He likes to find "sleepy *e*" words and "bossy *e*" words on My Spell Check. (For product information, see page 87.)

42

LESSON 28
Verb Tense:
Yesterday, Today, and Tomorrow

 INTO

Introduce or reinforce the concept of action in the past, present, or future (verb tense) by writing the following sentence frame on the board: **Yesterday I _____ to school.** Write the words **walk** and **walked** under the blank. Have students read the sentence aloud twice, inserting each of the words. Ask students which word sounds right. Explain that when we talk or write about an action that has already happened, we often add **-ed** to the verb. Erase **yesterday** and replace it with **tomorrow**. Add **will** in front of **walk**. Ask students to think about how the word **tomorrow** changes the sentence. Read the sentence aloud, inserting the two possibilities. Have students discuss the appropriate response and why *will walk* makes sense. Explain that when we talk or write about an action that will take place sometime in the future, we often write the word *will* in front of the action word. If time permits, model another sentence: **I already _____ that Nintendo game**. Write **play** and **played** beneath the sentence. Discuss the choices. Change the sentence to read: **After school today, I _____ a Nintendo game** with choices **will play**, **play**, and **played** written underneath. Discuss the choices.

 **THROUGH**

Tell students that Wordy is having some fun changing action words to tell about things that already happened and things that have not yet happened. Ask students to listen to hear about Wordy's actions. Read the poem aloud several times. Discuss Wordy's actions and what he has to do before he can *play* and *bake* again.

> **Yesterday, Today, and Tomorrow**
> Yesterday we played all day.
>   Tomorrow we will play some more.
> Today I cannot play at all,
>   Until I clean the bedroom floor.
>
> Yesterday we baked a lot.
>   Tomorrow we will bake some more.
> Today I cannot bake at all,
>   Until I clean the kitchen floor.

Distribute copies of Blackline Master 28. Have students follow along, join in, and identify key words as you guide them through several choral readings. Discuss the "cause-and-effect" relationship between the actions and the results. Ask students to find the -ed endings and explain why they occur. Do the same with the phrases using **will**.

Call attention to Wordy's actions in the illustration next to the poem. Ask students to describe what Wordy must do before he can *play* and *bake*.

Read Wordy's talk bubble request together: *"Your turn! Be sure your action word matches the day."* Do the first sentence as a group, modeling how to look for clues to determine the right word to fill in the blank. Read the other sentences together. Have students complete the insertions. Now read the three sentences at the bottom of the page and have students draw a star, check mark, or circle beside the appropriate sentence.

 **BEYOND**

This activity focuses attention on simple verb tenses, often a challenge for young writers. (*Word-Wise Sourcebook Two* deals with irregular verb tenses.) The following experiences may be useful for your students:

1. **What's Missing?** Use a familiar big book or chart poem selection. Tape an index card over the regular verb in a sentence. Ask students to provide the appropriate action word and to explain when the action takes, took, or will take place.

2. **Before and After:** Present able students with several sentences in which they must change the verb form from past to future, or vice versa. Sentences might include:

    I *jumped* over the rope; I *will talk* to my Grandma; My Mom *will show* me how to do it; My Dad *worked* on our car.

3. **Yesterday/Tomorrow:** Have students fold their lined paper into halves, heading one column **Yesterday** and the other **Tomorrow**. Put a list of familiar words on the board. Students write the appropriate verb tense for each column. Words might include: *help, ask, look, fish, call, show, jump.*

LESSON 29
Homophones:
Sound Alikes

 INTO

Oh, those crazy words that sound alike but don't look alike! No wonder they confuse Wordy. No wonder they confuse your emerging writers.

This lesson includes some of the most familiar of these tricky words called *homophones.*

To introduce or reinforce the concept of homophones, write the following sentences on the board: **I eight all ate pieces of candy. Then I new I wood feel sick.** Tell students that Wordy has found some words that are giving him a problem. Ask students to read the sentences silently to see if they can discover Wordy's problem words. Encourage them to conclude that some words sound alike but mean different things and are spelled differently. Ask for volunteers to fix the sentences on the board. Ask how they knew to switch *eight* and *ate* and how they knew to change *new* and *wood*. Write on the board: *Do you* **no** *(know) any* **pears** *(pairs) of words that confuse you when you* **right** *(write) them down?* Discuss the homophones.

 THROUGH

Explain that students will hear many words in Wordy's poem that sound alike but mean different things and are spelled differently. Ask them to listen carefully for these confusing words. Read the poem aloud several times.

> **Sound Alikes**
> You know those words that sound alike,
>   Like **eight** and **ate**, or **see** and **sea**?
> Sometimes I don't know how to spell—
>   These words are just confusing me!
>
> Like **four** and **for**, or **sun** and **son**,
>   Like **knew** and **new**, or **be** and **bee**?
> Sometimes I don't know how to spell—
>   These words are just confusing me!

Ask again why some of these words are confusing to Wordy. Have students recall words from the poem and write these homophones on the board. Explain that students will read these words when they get their own copy of Wordy's poem.

Distribute copies of Blackline Master 29. Have students follow along, join in, and identify key words as you guide them through several choral readings.

Call attention to the illustration next to the poem. Ask students what advice they would give Wordy about his spellings (**eight** should become **ate**; **pair** should become **pear**).

Have students join you in reading aloud the directions in Wordy's talk bubble: *"Your turn! Write the correct word."* Go over the sentence frames and the word choices to fill in the blanks. Ask students how they will know which word is the right spelling (*the word clues around the missing word*). Suggest that students complete the page independently or with a partner.

 BEYOND

This lesson on homophones also points out the importance of being a "word detective" and looking for word clues to help decide the spelling of a word. The following activities provide additional practice:

1. **Match Up:** Prepare (or have students prepare) word cards with pairs of homophones. Distribute the cards among students and have them find their "sounds like" partner. Once they have found a match, have them share their pair with the class, either defining their words, or using them in a sentence.

2. **Find the Word Pairs:** The following story can be read aloud so that students can identify pairs of homophones, or it can be put on the board or a worksheet. Ask students to see how many word pairs they can identify by underlining the words that sound alike.

   Mom said, "Let's go to see the sea this summer."

   "Oh, no," said Dad. "I know we will have to buy a new car."

   "I knew it," said Mom. "By the time you look at new cars, summer will be over. Can't the four of us fly to the beach?"

"No way," said Dad. "We all weigh too much!"

3. **First Hand Up!** Ask students to use their sharpest ears as you call out pairs of familiar homophones. Have students spell both homophones in the pair as you write them on the board.

> The Teaching Posters and Personal Posters in the Spelling Sourcebook Series remind Wordy Birdy which to use—there or their; to, too or two.

 INTO

Introduce or reinforce the concept of comparisons by asking students to let you borrow a pencil. Place the pencil in full view. Next ask volunteers to give you **bigger** pencils. Place the additional pencils in full view. Ask students to point to the biggest pencil. Do the same demonstration with crayons, asking for smaller and smaller crayons. Have students point to the smallest and the biggest. Explain that writers use comparing words to show differences between things. Continue to demonstrate using student volunteers: *Susie is taller than Samantha; Samantha is shorter than Susie . . . and Molly is shortest of all.*

 **THROUGH**

Explain that Wordy is having fun with some of these same words in a poem about his family. Have students listen to find out what Wordy has to say. Read the poem aloud several times.

> **Just the Right Word**
> I am big, but my brother is bigger,
>   My dad is the biggest of all!
> Dad's cookie is small,
>   and my brother's is smaller,
> But mine is the smallest of all!
>   **No fair!**

Discuss the things that Wordy is comparing in the poem. Tell students that they will have a chance to play with some of these words when they get their copy of Wordy's poem.

Distribute copies of Blackline Master 30. Have students follow along, join in, and identify key words as you guide them through several choral readings.

Call attention to Wordy and his family in the illustration. Ask students why Wordy looks unhappy.

Read the words in Wordy's talk bubble together: *"Your turn! Draw pictures to match the words!"* Go over each of the two sets of words, reading them aloud and asking students what pictures they might draw to show the differences, i.e., tall, taller, and tallest trees; short, shorter, and shortest box. Provide time for students to complete and share their pictures.

 **BEYOND**

This lesson introduces students to regularly formed comparison words. (*Word-Wise Sourcebook Two* works with irregular comparatives and superlatives.) To encourage the use of comparison words, try these activities:

1. **See-And-Compare:** Prepare sets of familiar comparing words on oak-tag strips and pass individual words out to students. Be sure the words have positive connotations. Ask for three student volunteers to come to the front of the class and arrange themselves in any order. Have students with labels come to the front of the room, match their label to a student, and use their word in a sentence, as in: *Jamie is bigger than Lincoln; Mark is shorter than Whitney;* etc.

2. **All About Me:** Put the following sentence frame on a worksheet or on the board:

   I am _____ than a _____,
   but I am _____ than a _____.

   Model the sentence, as in: *I am taller than a dog, but I am shorter than a building.* Encourage students to complete their own "All About Me" and to draw a picture illustrating their sentence.

3. **Stump Your Neighbor:** Have students draw three different-sized objects on a strip of construction paper. Objects can be the same or different as long as they are different sizes. Have students trade with a buddy and ask their partner to point to the small ____, the smaller ____, and the smallest ____.

Wordy Birdy and his friends like to practice using comparisons in Level 2 of the Spelling Sourcebook Series.

46

LESSON 31
Silent Letters: Where Did the Letters Go?

 INTO

Young students confront a real challenge when they first meet double-consonant combinations that have one silent letter. These combinations can appear anywhere in a word. Because words that have **kn** (knife), **wr** (wrap), **mb** (comb), **gh** (fight) are not spelled the way they are pronounced, students may need additional direct instruction in recognizing them.

Explain that Wordy is really confused and puzzled. Write **kite** and **kitten** on the board. Tell students that Wordy doesn't have any problems with these words because he knows that when **k** comes at the beginning of a word, it sounds like **c** in **cake**. Write **know** and **knee** on the board. Explain that these words are giving Wordy a hard time. Ask students to listen carefully as you pronounce these words. Ask what sound they hear at the beginning. Ask what letter sound they *don't* hear. Explain that when **kn** is in a word, the **k** is silent.

Write **cab**, **job**, and **tub** on the board. Read the words aloud emphasizing the sound of **b**. Have students tell you the sound that **b** makes in these words. Next, write **lamb**, **thumb**, and **comb** on the board. Repeat the sequence above.

 **THROUGH**

Tell students that Wordy has a poem about searching for sounds in words with silent letters. Ask students to listen for some tricky words. Read the poem aloud several times.

Discuss the differences in the words in the poem.

Distribute copies of Blackline Master 31. Have students follow along, join in, and identify new words as you guide them through several choral readings. Ask students to point to the letter in each word whose sound disappears when it is combined with another letter.

Call attention to Wordy Birdy's actions in the illustration next to the poem. Discuss what Wordy is doing to the word *thumb*. Explain that the correct spelling is t-h-u-m-b. Wordy has crossed out the silent letter to help him say the word.

Read Wordy's directions aloud: *"Your turn! Add silent letters to make the words. Use your new words in the sentences."* Complete the page together, or have students complete the page alone or with a partner.

 **BEYOND**

For extra practice and reinforcement, try these activities with silent letters:

1. **Advice for Wordy:** Write short lists of familiar words that have a silent partner in a double-consonant combination on the board. Ask students to examine these lists and decide what they can tell Wordy that will help him remember the right sounds. Guide them toward a generalization that will help Wordy.

2. **Silent Partner:** Distribute 3" x 5" index cards. Assign each student a familiar word that has

a **silent partner** in a double-consonant combination. Have students write a sentence with the word on the card and underline their word. Attach cards to a long piece of yarn. Hang the **silent partner** ladder in an accessible place for easy reference.

3. **Fix-Up:** Put the following paragraph on the board or on a worksheet. Encourage students to be proofreaders by reading the story carefully and changing any words that are misspelled.

> When I was little, I didn't no how to tie my shoelaces. Know I no how to do it. I would try to tie my laces the rong way. Know I no the write way.

Wordy Birdy likes to learn about letters that can't be heard in words. He collects and practices them in his Spelling Sourcebook activities. He uses his My Spell Check card to help him spell. (See page 87.)

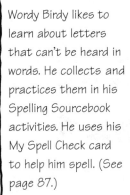

LESSON 32
Words that End in Y:
Tricky Little Y

 INTO

Introduce the concept that the letter **y** can represent different vowel sounds. Explain that Wordy Birdy is very confused about the letter you are writing on the board. Write **y** on the board. Tell students that Wordy doesn't have a problem when **y** is a consonant and comes at the beginning of words, like **you** and **yellow**. Ask students to think of other words that begin with the letter and sound of **y**. Again, mention that these words are no problem for Wordy.

 THROUGH

Write **fly** and **funny** on the board. Tell students that these words use the letter **y** at the end and that's when Wordy gets confused. Have students pronounce each word. Ask why they think Wordy might be confused *(because both words end in y but have a different ending sound)*. Encourage students to see that **y** has a different sound at the end of each word. Tell students that they are going to help Wordy figure out when to use each sound of **y**.

Under **fly**, write **try, my, by,** and **cry**. Under **funny**, write **any, family,** and **only**. Ask students to look carefully at each list of words to find what is different. Encourage students to observe that the short words often end in a long **i** sound of **y**; the longer words often end in a long **e** sound of

48

y. Have students clap out the syllables of the words in each list.

Ask students to listen to Wordy's poem to see what they now know that Wordy doesn't know. Read the poem aloud several times. Have students explain why the letter **y** sounds different at the end of each word. Tell students they will have more chances to help Wordy when they see their own copy of his poem.

> ### Tricky Little Y
>
> **Y** is such a tricky letter,
>> **Y** puts on a different sound.
>
> Every time I learn it better,
>> **Y** has changed its sound around.
>
> I've learned the sound of **y** in **try**,
>> The sound of **y** in **yellow**, too.
>
> But in other words like **baby**,
>> **Y** won't do what it should do!

Distribute copies of Blackline Master 32. Have students follow along, join in, and identify key words as you guide them through several choral readings.

Call attention to Wordy shaking his head in the illustration. Have a volunteer tell Wordy the trick for deciding on the sound of **y** at the end of words.

Find Wordy's talk bubble and read his request together: *"Your turn! Write the Y words where they belong!"* Read the words together. Explain that students are to read each word and write the word on the appropriate lines under "**Y** sounds like **i** saying its name" or "**Y** sounds like **e** saying its name."

 **BEYOND**

Young students may share Wordy's confusion with **y**-ending words. In the next level of this program, **y** is also presented as a medial vowel, as in **gym**. The following activities reinforce and provide practice with the sounds of **y**:

1. **Everybody Show:** Explain that the letter **y** wears many different costumes to try to fool us:
   - sometimes like the consonant **y** in **yellow**,
   - sometimes like the long **i** in **fly**, and
   - sometimes like the long **e** in **silly**.

   For a check on phonemic awareness, distribute three 1" x 1" cards to each student: one card has the letter **y**; the second card has the letter **i**; the third card has the letter **e**. As you call out a word, students are to listen carefully for the sound of **y**, place the appropriate card in their **Everybody Show** holder, and display the holder.

2. **Detective Search:** Ask students to be detectives as they read a familiar story. They are to search for words with **y** at the beginning or the end and make a list of these words. Provide time for students to share their lists and discuss the different sounds.

3. **Tricky Y Chart:** Have students contribute to a three-column butcher-paper chart by writing in the appropriate column words that begin or end with **y**. Columns are headed: **Y at the beginning**; **Y sounds like i**; and **Y sounds like e**.

Tricky Y is not too tricky for Wordy! His Spelling Sourcebook activities help him with other tricky letters, too. Now Wordy knows the letters and the sounds they can spell. (See page 87.)

WORDY BIRDY PUPPET

QUEENIE QUESTION MARK

POLLY PERIOD

APPY APOSTROPHE

Wordy Birdy

My name is Wordy Birdy.
  I'm not like other birds.
They can sing and chirp and tweet,
  But I can play with WORDS!

That's why I'm Wordy Birdy.
  Just watch what I can do.
Follow me—if I can do it,
  You can do it, too!

Name _____

Words Around the Room

Walk around the room with me.
Count how many words you see!
Walking fast or walking slow,
What really **counts** are words you **know**!

Pick a Letter

Wordy Birdy picked a **b**
　　For babies, bananas, and bats,
Flew next door and picked a **c**
　　For coconuts, candy, and cats.

Your turn now to pick a letter,
　　Think of words that start the same.
Wordy knows you're getting better
　　At this Wordy Birdy game!

Your turn! Make pictures to match each beginning letter.

b	d

Name _____

Which Sound Do You Hear?

A – A – Annie
    is wearing a wig.
E – E – Eddie
    is riding a pig.
I – I – Izzy
    is dancing a jig.
O – O – Otto
    is eating a fig.
U – U – Umpty
    is holding a twig.

Your turn! Write the vowel
a, e, i, o, or **u** to spell
the words in each sentence.

The c__t is f__t.

A b__g is in a r__g.

Blackline Master 4

All in the Family

Please come to meet my family,
Mom and Grandma and Auntie Bee!
Look over here—four more to see,
My uncle, my cousin, my brother, and me!

Your turn! I want to meet your family!

Word Family Friends

Come over to meet the **an** family,
  Here's **m** and **r** and **c**.
And next to them is the **at** family,
  Here's **c** and **f** and **b**.

Be sure to meet the **ap** family,
  Here's **m** and **c** and **t**.
It's fun to meet word families,
  How many can you see?

Your turn! Write the name of each family member you met under its house.

an family   **at** family   **ap** family

man   cat   map

Blackline Master 6

Don't Call Me Wordy Piggy

Please don't call me **Wordy Piggy**!
That is not this birdy's name.
My mama said my name should be
Two words that sound the same.

Please don't call me **Birdy Yellow**,
Or **Wordy Once-Upon-A-Time**.
You must call me **Wordy Birdy**,
'Cause then my name will rhyme!

Your turn! Pick an animal word that makes a rhyme. Then draw a picture of your animal in the box.

A funny _____
cat   mouse   bunny

A fat _____
cow   cat   dog

Name ______________________________

Color Me Pink

Wordy fell into the bathtub.
Wordy fell into the sink.
Wordy fell into the cherry jam
And came out **pink**!

Wordy fell into the bucket.
Wordy fell into the bed.
Wordy fell into the berry jam
And came out **red**!

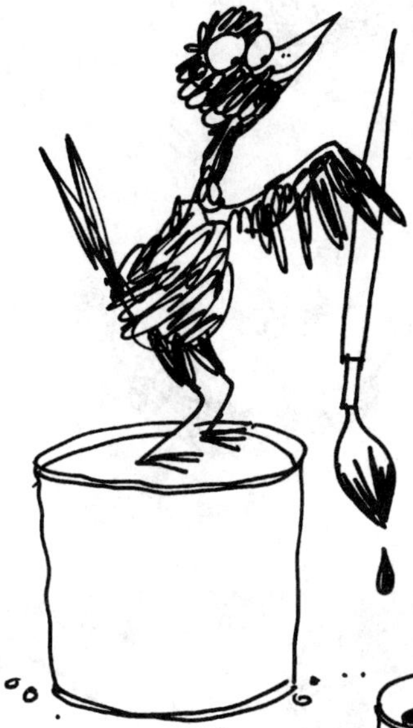

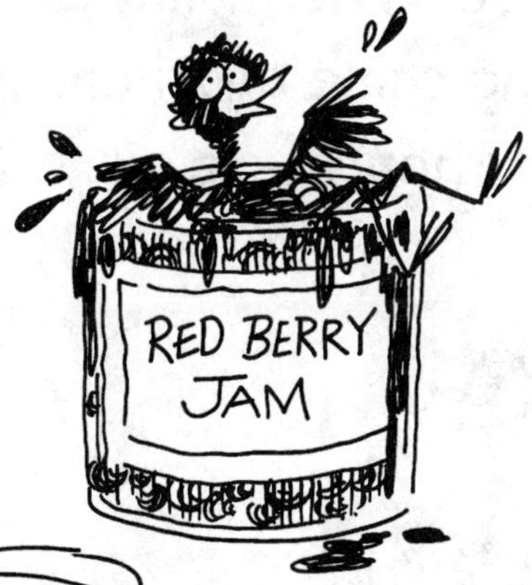
RED BERRY
JAM

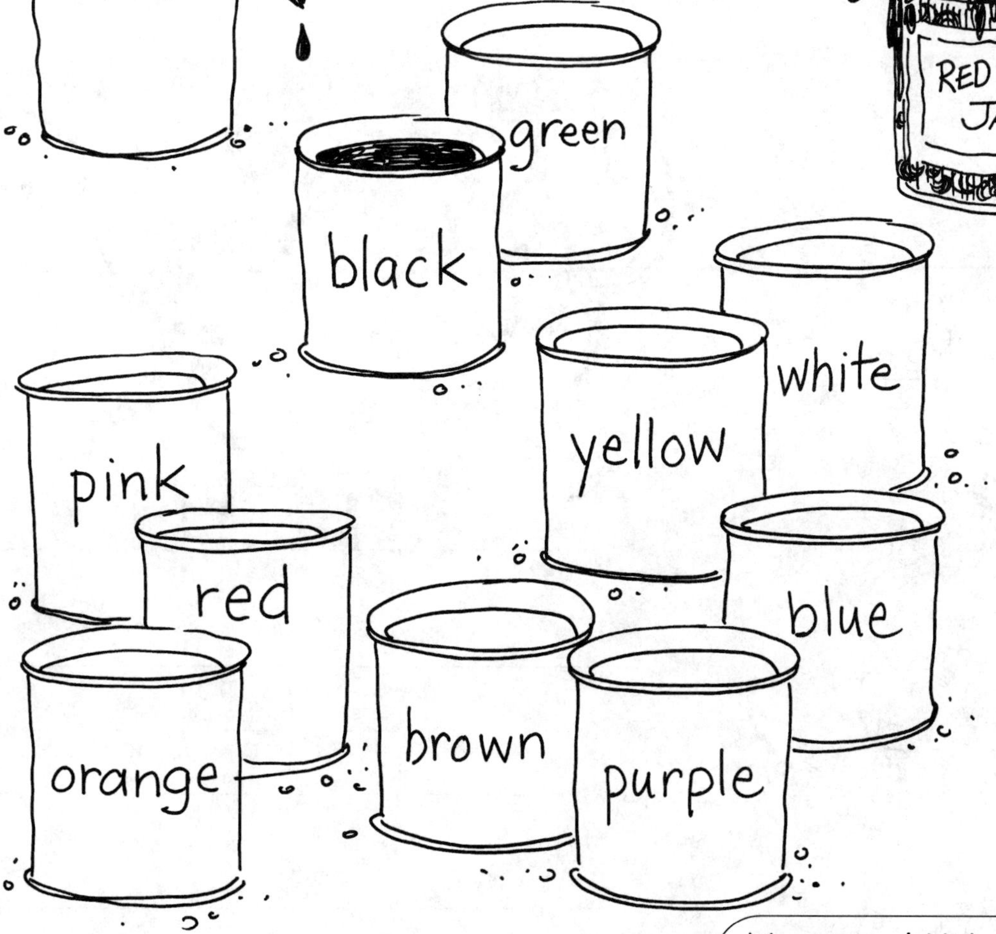
green
black
white
yellow
pink
red
blue
brown
orange
purple

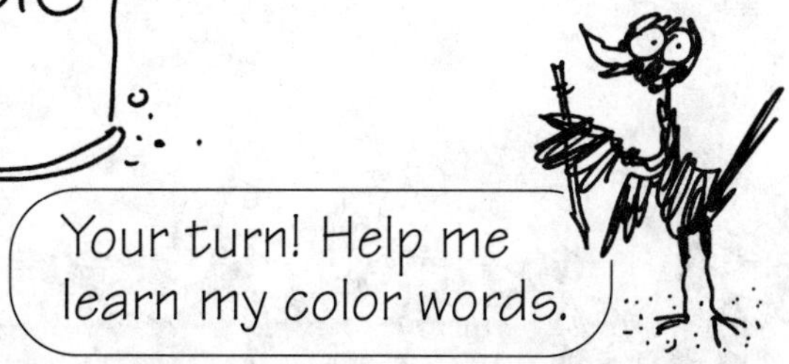
Your turn! Help me
learn my color words.

Name _____

Monkeying Around

One little monkey tying her shoe;
Along came another,
And then there were two.

Two little monkeys drinking some tea;
Along came another,
And then there were three.

Three little monkeys banging on a door;
Along came another,
And then there were four.

Your turn! Help me
count these monkeys.

three
_____
_ _
_____

_____
_ _
_____

_____
_ _
_____

Name _____

The Animals Have the Sillies Today

The animals have
   The sillies today.
The animals talk
   In the funniest way.

"Peep," says the duck.
"Squeak," says the cat.
"Quack," says the chick.
"Meow," says the rat.

 Your turn! Let's help these silly animals.
Put the right sound in each talk bubble
and the animal name on the line.

_____

- -

_____

_____

- -

_____

_____

- -

_____

_____

- -

_____

Name _____

Macaroni

Macaroni, macaroni,
That's the stuff for me.
Macaroni, macaroni,
Messy as can be.

Your turn! Think of your favorite messy food. Make a picture of it in this box.

_____   _____
- - - - - - - - - - - - - - - - - -   - - - - - - - - - - - - - - - - - -
_____ ,   _____ ,

That's the stuff for me.

_____   _____
- - - - - - - - - - - - - - - - - -   - - - - - - - - - - - - - - - - - -
_____ ,   _____ ,

Messy as can be.

Name _____

Who Thinks Up Names?

Who thinks up all the names for things—
  Like pencil, paper, desk, and book,
And airplane, bus, and ten-speed bike?
  Wow! Think of all the time it took!

Who thinks up all the names for places—
  Stores and cities, rivers, too?
Who thinks up names for schools and streets?
  I know it wasn't me or you!

Who thinks up all the names for people,
  So they won't all be the same?
At least I know who named me **Wordy**.
  Thank you, Papa, for my name!

> Your turn! Be sure to name
> the things in your pictures!

A Person	A Place	A Thing

_____   _____   _____

-------------------   -------------------   -------------------

_____   _____   _____

Name _____

Funny Bunny, Fat Cat

Funny Bunny!
Jump, run,
Hide, hop,
Sniff, chew,
Never stop.
Funny Bunny!

Fat Cat!
Chase, claw,
Scratch, hiss,
Race, meow,
Jump, miss.
Fat Cat!

Your turn! Write the words that tell what **I** can do and the words that tell what **you** can do.

Wordy can

_____

_____

_____

_____

_____

sing

fly

play

I can

_____

_____

_____

_____

_____

I Saw . . .

I saw a cat.
I saw a big cat.
I saw a big, white cat.
I saw a big, white, hissing cat.
I saw a big, white, hissing cat chasing.
I saw a big, white, hissing cat chasing me.
   I'm out of here!

Your turn! Make a poem like mine
that tells about something.

_____
- -

I saw a _____.

_____   _____
- - - - - - - - - - - - - -   - - - - - - - - - - - - - -

I saw a _____   _____.

_____ _____ _____
- - - - - - - - - - - - - - - - - - - - - - - - - - - - - -

I saw a _____ _____ _____.

Name _____

Wordy Birdy, Wordy Birdy

Wordy Birdy, Wordy Birdy, turn around.
Wordy Birdy, Wordy Birdy, touch the ground.
Wordy Birdy, Wordy Birdy, count to three.
Wordy Birdy, Wordy Birdy, touch your knee.

Your turn! Follow the directions!

Make a blue circle.

N		s
M		t
P		p
R		w
B		n
T		r
S		m
W		b

Match the letters.

Draw a face.

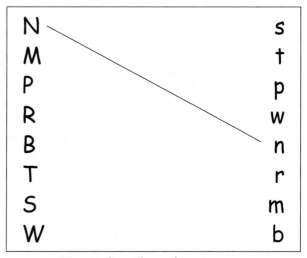

I saw . . .

a dog on a log.

a fish in a dish.

a bird in a hat.

a pig in a wig.

Circle the rhyming words.

Macaroni #2

Macaroni, macaroni,
That's the stuff for me.
Macaroni, macaroni,
Messy as can be.

Do I have it on my jeans?
Yes, you have it on your jeans!

Do I have it on my shirt?
Yes, you have it on your shirt!

Do I have it on my shoes?
Yes, you have it on your shoes!

Your turn! Fill in the missing words. See
if you can put **Queenie Question Mark**
(?) and **Polly Period** (.) in the right place.

What is your name _____

_____

_____

My name is _____ _____

How old are you _____

_____

_____

I am _____ years old _____

Name _____

Two Words in One

Football, snowman, cowgirls, too,
Look at what these words can do!
They go together for a start,
Or we can take these words apart!

 Your turn! Match the words that go
together. Write your new word on the line.

play   self   _____

bath   side   _____

foot   tub   **bathtub**

in   ground   _____

my   ball   _____

Name _____

What Do They Say?

HE'S a HE; HE'S not a WE,
And SHE is not an IT.
And sometimes I am only ME.
When does the right word fit?

I know that WE are not a THEM,
And THEM is sometimes THEY,
But how 'bout YOU and HER and HIM?
Who knows what's right to say?

Your turn! Make some
pictures that match.

we	**me**

she	**he**

Name _____

Just the Opposite

Wordy says **yes**. You say **no**!

Wordy says **stop**. You say **go**!

Wordy says **fast**. You say **slow**!

Wordy says fly. You say NO WAY!

Your turn! I'll say the word and you say the opposite.

sad   day   in   down

_____

Wordy says **night**. You say _____.

Wordy says **up**. You say _____.

Wordy says **happy**. You say _____.

Wordy says **out**. You say _____.

Watch Them Grow

Plant a word! It's fun to try.
You need a verb to start.
Watch it grow to other words.
I knew that you were smart!

Let's show you how a word can grow,
Let's plant a word like **play**.
It sprouts to **playing**, **played**, **replayed**.
What others can you say?

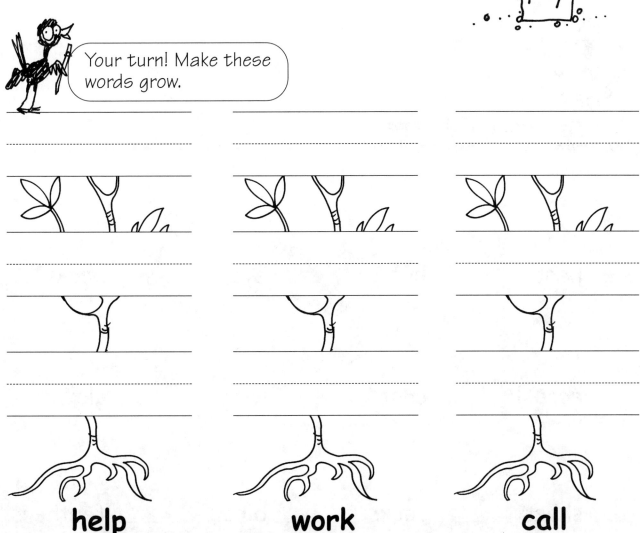

Your turn! Make these words grow.

help   **work**   **call**

One Shoe, Two Shoes

One shoe, two shoes,
Red shoes, blue shoes,
  Shoes that slide,
  Shoes that ride.

One shoe, two shoes,
White shoes, blue shoes,
  Shoes that run,
  Shoes for fun.

head   hat   eyes   beak   gloves   wings   coat   socks   shoes

Your turn! Write 1 if the word names one thing. Write 2 if the word names more than one thing.

_____ head   _____ hat   _____ eyes   _____ beak

_____ ears   _____ coat   _____ wings   _____ gloves

_____ shoes   _____ socks   _____ bird   _____ feathers

Tricky Words

A kitty can lap some milk,
And I can lap a mile,
But sitting on my mama's lap
Can really make me smile!

My daddy cans some peaches,
And I can can some, too.
We can them in a gallon can,
It's really fun to do.

Your turn! The word is spelled the same but the meaning is different! Write the word **run** in each blank space.

Run

_____

"Run, _____, as fast as you can.

You can't catch me—I'm the gingerbread man!"

My friend can hit a home _____.

A cold makes my nose _____.

Say It Better

Some words are old. Put them away!
Let's use some other words today.

Instead of **big**, say **huge** or **wide**.
Instead of **said**, think **shouted**, **cried**.

Instead of **little**, why not **tiny**?
Pick words that sparkle, new and shiny!

Your turn! Think of another
word that means the same.

Old   New

little   small

bad   _____

walked   _____

good   _____

tall   _____

Name _____

Taking Shortcuts

You say **do not**. I say **don't**.
You say **will not**. I say **won't**.
Which is quicker? Which is fast?
Take a shortcut—don't be last!

don't

Your turn! Put **Appy Apostrophe** (')
where he belongs!

_____

_____ my birthday!
It is

I _____ watch TV tonight.
cannot

_____ my best friend.
You are

_____ going to Disneyland!
We are

Name _____

Can You Find Me?

Can you find me?
I'm easy to see.
I'm in wiggle and giggle,
And bee and tree.

I'm in look and book,
And little and fiddle.
If I'm not at the end,
I'll be in the middle.

 Your turn! Use these double letters to spell the words in my poem.

ee   tt   nn   ll

Molly likes bu__ __ons;
She doesn't like bows.

Molly likes f__ __t;
She doesn't like toes.

Molly likes je__ __y;
She doesn't like jam.

Molly likes De__ __y;
She doesn't like Sam.

Wordy's Blending Sounds Today

Wordy's blending sounds today;
He says it's fun to do.

Wordy's blending sounds today;
He has some words for you.

Flee, fly, flew;
  Black, blond, blue;
Green, grow, grew;
  Stop, stamp, stew.

Your turn! Use the letters to make a new word. Write your new word on the line.

fl   dr   bl   st   cr

A __ __y is in my __ __ink,

A big __ __ack __ __y!

Get it out! Get it out!

Or I will __ __art to __ __y.

Name _____

"E" on the End—A Silent Friend

Tricky little "no sound" **e**
Sitting on the end.
Keeping quiet, keeping still,
What message do you send?

Your turn! Don't forget
to add the silent **e**!

Can you bak__ a cak__?

I can mak__ a fac__.

Can you rid__ a bik__?

I can tell the tim__.

Yesterday, Today, and Tomorrow

Yesterday we played all day.
  Tomorrow we will play some more.
Today I cannot play at all,
  Until I clean the bedroom floor.

Yesterday we baked a lot.
  Tomorrow we will bake some more.
Today I cannot bake at all,
  Until I clean the kitchen floor.

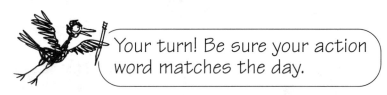

Your turn! Be sure your action word matches the day.

Use **walk**, **walked**, or **will walk** in the right sentence.

_____

Yesterday I _____ to school.

Right now I can _____ around the field.

Tomorrow I _____ with my friend.

★ Put a star beside the sentence that tells about something you have already done.

✓ Put a check beside the sentence that tells about something you do now.

○ Put a circle beside the sentence that tells about something you will do the next day.

Blackline Master 28

Sound Alikes

You know those words that sound alike,
  Like **eight** and **ate**, or **see** and **sea**?
Sometimes I don't know how to spell—
  These words are just confusing me!

Like **four** and **for**, or **sun** and **son**,
  Like **knew** and **new**, or **be** and **bee**?
Sometimes I don't know how to spell—
  These words are just confusing me!

Your turn! Write the correct word.

I _____ the race.

       one   won

I didn't _____ I could run so fast.

       no   know

I can fill in the _____ word.

       right   write

_____ how easy it is?

  Sea   See

Name _____

Just the Right Word

I am big, but my brother is bigger,
  My dad is the biggest of all!
Dad's cookie is small,
  and my brother's is smaller,
But mine is the smallest of all!
No fair!

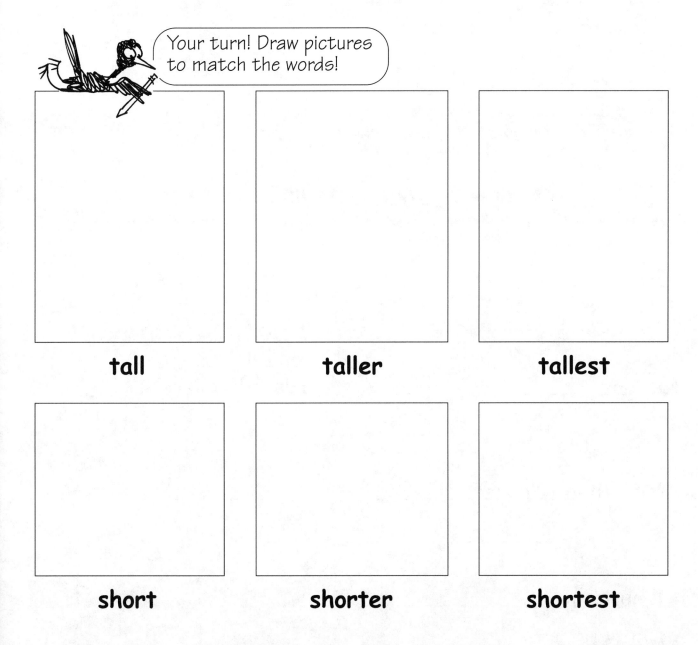

Your turn! Draw pictures to match the words!

tall   **taller**   **tallest**

short   **shorter**   **shortest**

Where Did the Letters Go?

Wordy has a problem,
  A problem with a word.
He hears the sound of **k** in **kite**,
  In **knob**, **k** can't be heard.

Wordy has a problem,
  A problem with a word.
He hears the sound of **b** in **crab**,
  In **lamb**, **b** can't be heard.

Your turn! Add silent letters to make the words. Use your new words in the sentences.

_now   _not   thum_   lam_

_____

- -

I have a _____ in my shoelace.

_____

- -

I _____ my ABCs.

_____

- -

Mary had a little _____.

_____

- -

I hurt my _____.

Name _____

Tricky Little Y

Y is such a tricky letter,
  Y puts on a different sound.
Every time I learn it better,
  Y has changed its sound around.

I've learned the sound of **y** in **try**,
  The sound of **y** in **yellow**, too.
But in other words like **baby**,
  Y won't do what it should do!

Your turn! Write the **Y** words where they belong!

fry   **many**   **by**   **any**   **sky**   **unhappy**   **messy**   **cry**

Y sounds like i saying its name

_____   _____

_____   _____

_____   _____

_____   _____

Y sounds like e saying its name

_____   _____

_____   _____

_____   _____

_____   _____

Blackline Master Answer Key

Word-Wise Sourcebook One   Additional answers may apply.

1 Wordy Birdy
   cat bat dog frog

2 Words Around the Room
   Pictures and words will vary.

3 Pick a Letter
   Pictures will vary.

4 Which Sound Do You Hear?
   cat fat bug rug

5 All in the Family
   Family pictures will vary.

6 Word Family Friends
   man, ran, can   cat, fat, bat   map, cap, tap

7 Don't Call Me Wordy Piggy
   Pictures will vary; A funny bunny; A fat cat

8 Color Me Pink
   Colors should match labels.

9 Monkeying Around
   three   five   six

10 The Animals Have the Sillies Today
   quack (duck)   meow (cat)
   peep (chick)   squeak (rat)

11 Macaroni
   Food pictures and words will vary.

12 Who Thinks Up Names?
   Pictures and words will vary.

13 Funny Bunny, Fat Cat
   Wordy can   sing, fly, play
   I can   sing, play

14 I Saw . . .
   Words will vary.

15 Wordy Birdy, Wordy Birdy
   Artwork should match labels;
   dog   log
   fish   dish
   pig   wig

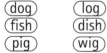

16 Macaroni #2
   ?   Names will vary.
   ?   Ages will vary.

17 Two Words in One
   myself inside bathtub playground
   football

18 What Do They Say?
   Artwork should match labels.

19 Just the Opposite
   day down sad in

20 Watch Them Grow
   Answers will vary; these may appear:
   helped, helper, helping, helps, helpful,
   helpless
   worked, worker, rework, working, works
   called, caller, recall, calling, calls

21 One Shoe, Two Shoes
   1 head   1 hat   2 eyes   1 beak
   2 ears   1 coat   2 wings   2 gloves
   2 shoes   2 socks   1 bird   2 feathers

22 Tricky Words
   run run run

23 Say It Better
   Answers will vary; these may appear:
   itty-bitty, small, teensy, tiny
   awful, mean, ornery, terrible
   paced, strode, strolled, strutted
   great, nice, super, terrific, wonderful
   gigantic, lofty, soaring, towering

24 Taking Shortcuts
   It's   can't You're We're

25 Can You Find Me?
   buttons feet jelly Denny

26 Wordy's Blending Sounds Today
   fly drink black fly start cry

27 "E" on the End—A Silent Friend
   bake cake make face ride bike time

28 Yesterday, Today and Tomorrow
   * walked   √ walk   ○ will walk

29 Sound Alikes
   won   know   right   See

30 Just the Right Word
   Artwork should match labels.

31 Where Did the Letters Go?
   know   knot   thumb   lamb
   knot   know   lamb   thumb

32 Tricky Little Y
   fry   sky   by   cry
   many   happy   any   messy

86

**Rebecca Sitton's
SPELLING SOURCEBOOK® Series,
2nd edition ©2002**

The all new SPELLING SOURCEBOOK Series for grades 1-8 provides the infrastructure to craft a spelling program your way. Opportunities to teach, practice, and apply all the traditional skills and concepts are included in this completely revised edition of the teacher-friendly, easy-to-manage series. One teacher resource book for each level contains everything you need—how to put it together day-by-day, unit-by-unit, from the beginning of the year to the end. You're in charge! Select the activities, tests, and blackline masters in every unit to create a balanced program that's right for you and your students. You'll see the results where spelling really counts—in students' everyday writing!

- Extensive menu of activities to choose from in every unit for teaching basic skills and concepts.
- Testing options—cloze (fill-in-the-blanks) story, sentence dictation, skill, and proof-reading (Levels 5-8) tests in every unit; periodic achievement tests to assess spelling progress.
- Blackline masters including take-home tasks in every unit to encourage parent-child partnerships.
- Opportunities for integration—language and literature tie-ins.
- Five new Teaching Posters to target instruction at every level included in each SPELLING SOURCEBOOK.

WORD-WISE SOURCEBOOKS™ ©2003

Your source for the best of Dr. Barbara Schmidt's and Dr. Maurice Poe's laugh-aloud rhymes for learning spelling and language skills. Separate blackline masters for 32 poems and activities guide students through spelling and language acquisition.
- Word-Wise Sourcebook One for Grades 1-2
- Word-Wise Sourcebook Two for Grades 3-4
- Word-Wise Sourcebook Three for Grades 5-6

SEMINAR HANDBOOK
Increasing Student Spelling Achievement
Your source for follow-along use during live training seminars and for reference after the seminar. Contains over 100 pages of reference information, including the top 1200 high-use writing words.

OVERVIEW VIDEO

Call 888-937-7355 (toll-free) to request our FREE Overview Video Package. The on-loan video and accompanying material make it easy to determine if this is the right approach for your class, school, or district. It is an ideal informational tool to share with colleagues to introduce them to the SPELLING SOURCEBOOK Series.

TEACHING POSTERS
(packaged with each Sourcebook)
Each Sourcebook comes with five colorful 18" x 24" grade level specific teaching posters to complement instruction. Replacement sets are available for purchase.

100 WORD WALL CHART
(appropriate for all grades)
Your classroom source for the alphabetical listing of the top 100 high-use writing words. Each package contains five copies of this useful 18" x 24" chart.

MY SPELL CHECK® K-2 (pkg. of 10)
(suggested for students in grades K-2)
Your students' source for an alphabetical listing of 85 high-use writing words, with sections for animals, numbers, family, clothes, school, days, months, foods, and weather. Each coated card is 8 1/2" x 11", in color on both sides. Package includes a teacher resource of over 50 spelling and writing activities. Packaged in sets of 10 cards with activities sheet.

SPELL CHECK® 3-8 (pkg. of 10)
(suggested for students in grades 3-8)
Your students' source for an alphabetical listing of 150 high-use writing words, with references for months, days of the week, common abbreviations, and 75 context sentences for often-confused words. Each coated card is 8 1/2" x 11", in color on both sides. Package includes a teacher resource of over 50 spelling and writing activities to extend the high-use word bank. Packaged in sets of 10 cards with activities sheet.

NEW PRODUCTS

COMING IN 2003:
CORE WORD ACTIVITY CARDS
Cards for posting/practice of high-use words, with skill-based lessons for every Core Word in Levels 1-3.

WORD SKILLS IN RHYTHM AND RHYME
Interactive CDs for Levels 1-3—an immensely motivational approach for learning essential skills.

**Rebecca Sitton's
SPELLING SOURCEBOOK® Series
©2002**
published by Egger Publishing, Inc.
P.O. Box 12248, Scottsdale, AZ 85267
888-WE-SPELL (888-937-7355)
fax 480-951-2276
Find us on the web at www.sittonspelling.com
Contact Rebecca at 480-473-7277
e-mail: rsitton@sittonspelling.com

Materials Description

WHERE TO SEND YOUR ORDER

TEXAS only
DDS Southwest
600 Freeport Parkway • Coppell, TX 75019
800-266-5122 • fax 214-452-6301

ALL OTHERS
Northwest Textbook Depository
P.O. Box 5608 • Portland, OR 97228
800-676-6630 • fax 503-639-2559

Thanks for your order!
Please call Egger Publishing
with program questions—
toll free 888-WE-SPELL.
(937-7355)
Every child a speller!

Order Form   Rebecca Sitton's SPELLING SOURCEBOOK® Series

SPELLING SOURCEBOOKS—2nd Edition ©2002

	PRICE	QTY.	TOTAL
GRADE 1—41-10002	$99.00		
(includes 5 teaching posters for Grade 1)			
GRADE 2—41-10003	$109.00		
(includes 5 teaching posters for Grade 2)			
GRADE 3—41-10004	$115.00		
(includes 5 teaching posters for Grade 3)			
GRADE 4—41-10005	$115.00		
(includes 5 teaching posters for Grade 4)			
GRADE 5—41-10006	$115.00		
(includes 5 teaching posters for Grade 5)			
GRADE 6—41-10007	$115.00		
(includes 5 teaching posters for Grade 6)			
GRADE 7—41-10008	$115.00		
(includes 5 teaching posters for Grade 7)			
GRADE 8—41-10009	$115.00		
(includes 5 teaching posters for Grade 8)			

ADDITIONAL BOOKS

Increasing Student Spelling Achievement

	PRICE	QTY.	TOTAL
Seminar Handbook	$10.00		
Word-Wise Sourcebook™ One—41-17108	$42.50		
Grades 1–2 (Wordy Birdy)			
Word-Wise Sourcebook™ Two—41-17109	$42.50		
Grades 3–4 (Willy Wordster)			
Word-Wise Sourcebook™ Three—41-17110	$42.50		
Grades 5–6 (Inspector Clue-So)			

NEW PRODUCTS COMING IN 2003

CORE WORD ACTIVITY CARDS for posting and practice of high-use words—with skill-based lessons for every Core Word in Levels 1-3.

WORD SKILLS IN RHYTHM AND RHYME interactive CDs for Levels 1-3—an immensely motivational approach for learning essential skills.

TEACHING AIDS

	PRICE	QTY.	TOTAL
TEACHING POSTERS			
Replacement posters for the Spelling Sourcebooks			
(one set is included with each Sourcebook)			
set of 5 grade-specific posters			
GRADE 1—41-10010	$9.50		
GRADE 2—41-10011	$9.50		
GRADE 3—41-10012	$9.50		
GRADE 4—41-10013	$9.50		
GRADE 5—41-10014	$9.50		
GRADE 6—41-10015	$9.50		
GRADE 7—41-10016	$9.50		
GRADE 8—41-10017	$9.50		
WALL CHARTS—41-10018	$8.50		
Top 100 High-Use Writing Words (5-pack)			
Appropriate for all grades			
STUDENT SPELL CHECK CARDS			
My Spell Check® K-2 (10-pack)—41-20103	$5.50		
With teacher resource of over 50 word activity ideas			
Spell Check® 3-8 (10-pack)—41-20104	$5.50		
With teacher resource of over 50 word activity ideas			

POSTAGE AND HANDLING

	U.S.	Canada
$0–$49	$4.00	$8.00
$50–499	8%	14%
$500–999	$40.00	$70.00
$1000 +	4%	7%

Subtotal	
Tax (CA 8.0%, WA 8.6%)	
Postage/Handling	
TOTAL	

ALL PRICES SUBJECT TO CHANGE WITHOUT NOTICE.

Purchase Order No. _____

Account No.: _____

☐ Check ☐ Visa ☐ MasterCard exp. date _____

Authorized Signature: _____

BILL TO:

School/District: _____

Attention: _____

Address: _____

City/State/ZIP: _____

Phone: _____

FAX: _____

SHIP TO:

School/Attn.: _____

_____

Address: _____

City/State/ZIP: _____

Phone: _____

FAX: _____